ALL THAT MATTERS

Sir Chris Hoy

**HODDER &
STOUGHTON**

First published in Great Britain in 2024 by Hodder & Stoughton Limited
An Hachette UK company

1

Copyright © Sir Chris Hoy 2024
Written with Matt Majendie

A CIP catalogue record for this title is available from the British Library

Hardback ISBN 9781399741842
Trade paperback ISBN 9781399741859
ebook ISBN 9781399741873

Typeset in Minion Pro by Palimpsest Book Production Limited,
Falkirk, Stirlingshire

Printed and bound in Great Britain by Clays Ltd, Elcograf S.p.A.

Hodder & Stoughton policy is to use papers that are natural, renewable and recyclable
products and made from wood grown in sustainable forests. The logging and manufacturing
processes are expected to conform to the environmental regulations of the country of origin.

Hodder & Stoughton Limited
Carmelite House
50 Victoria Embankment
London EC4Y 0DZ

The authorised representative in the EEA is Hachette Ireland,
8 Castlecourt Centre, Castleknock Road, Castleknock,
Dublin 15, D15 YF6A, Ireland
(email: info@hbgi.ie)

www.hodder.co.uk

For Sarra, Callum and Chloe

PROLOGUE

THERE'S a pain in my shoulder. It's occasional at first, and then constant – there first thing in the morning and still niggling away at me last thing at night. It's nothing exceptional, the sort of aches and pains I've grown accustomed to when pushing myself in the gym and on the bike.

Perhaps this is the way things are now. At forty-seven, are these the first signs of getting old? Am I kidding myself, still squatting 200 kilograms in fitness sessions? Is it time to start slowing down and not revert to being an Olympic athlete every time I step into the gym? During my cycling career, I was always proud of my high pain threshold – my ability to push myself beyond the limits, never having to use painkillers – but this isn't going away, even with some physiotherapy and rest.

Paracetamol helps initially to dull the pain, but slowly the effect of that begins to wear off. Now, after two weeks, it's barely making a dent in the constant ache that's there every waking moment and each time I roll over in bed at night. Occasionally, the thought pops into my head that there might be something more sinister at play here, but I quickly dismiss it. I know what's wrong really, what a scan will tell me: it's simply a case of tendonitis in my shoulder. As a professional sportsman, you have enough bangs and injury setbacks to make you understand your body, almost enabling you to self-diagnose. My physiotherapist refers me for a scan, and as I walk to the hospital entrance I predict in my head the conversation playing out – I'll simply be told to lay off any upper-body work in the gym for a couple of weeks and get some follow-up treatment. More than a decade into retirement, maybe it's simply time to slow down.

It's amazing, on reflection, how wrong I could be.

CHAPTER ONE

SEPTEMBER 2023

AFTER the scan, I step into the doctor's office for the results, feeling unconcerned and keen to get this pain sorted. There's a vague smell of sanitised surfaces, the typical bright lights of a hospital room flickering and humming overhead, a few papers stacked loosely on the table; and there, next to a computer, is a doctor, slowly raising his head to look at me as I enter the room. But he's not alone for this consultation: to one side sits a nurse. Her presence both spikes my curiosity and sets off the first slight alarm bells in my head, causing a shift in my mentality from this simply being gym wear and tear to something more ominous.

My immediate thought is, *Why have they brought someone else in for this?* But before I have time for further internal questioning, the doctor comes out with it:

'I'm really sorry. There's a tumour in your shoulder.'

My blood turns to ice. He's talking, the words spilling out from his mouth about another scan being booked in at the oncology department, about the next steps. He mentions the Christie Hospital, a name I know – it's well known in the

North West as a centre of excellence for cancer care – but either I don't really hear him or most of the subsequent words simply don't sink in. I'm in a state of shock. I can't get a grip on his words or the room. A tumour. So far from what was on my list of possible causes.

Then he turns the screen to me to reveal the scan in all its grainy detail and the tumour that, unbeknown to the me of an hour ago, is currently in my shoulder. How long it's resided there, I have no idea, but I don't want to look at it, as though laying my eyes on it might make it more real and horrific than it already is. I turn away, not quite willing to accept this news just yet. How can I? It's beyond comprehension. Hearing the word 'cancer' has had an immediate and profound effect on me, and not just me. Next to the doctor, the nurse's eyes fill with tears.

My medical self-diagnosis has been so, so wrong.

It's akin to having the wind knocked out of me, a sensory overload that leaves me in a total daze. I have never felt anything like this before. One moment to the next is a blur and then, before I know it, I'm up and out of the chair, the appointment over, and, zombie-like, I turn the handle of the office door and head back down the corridors. In one short moment, life has changed irrevocably.

Before the appointment, I'd planned on taking a taxi home, but, without really engaging my brain, I find myself out of the hospital doors and then just walking and walking and walking on this late September day. I have a world of thoughts circulating around my brain, yet none of what's just unfolded seems real.

The walk home must be about five miles in all, and there's a moment during it when it hits me like a breeze block: *oh my God, what will I tell Sarra?* That's when the first wave of emotion really hits. Step by step, I slowly get my head around it, trying to be rational about news that has struck me like a sledge hammer. I take a deep breath and I ring her. She's gone to a friend's house nearby for a catch-up while I'm at the doctor's appointment. 'What happened at the scan?' she asks. But in the moment, I fudge it, I can't get the words out, not when she isn't with me, and 'I'll tell you later' I say, trying to sound unconcerned rather than shell-shocked.

Sarra says she's heading off and she'll see me at home. I hang up, thought after thought continuing to race through my head. But then, suddenly, I snap out of my mind and back to reality as I notice Sarra – cheery, but clearly concerned – winding down the car window and waving as she drives past me at the bottom of the road to our house. I can see that she knows something's wrong. Even if it wasn't something of this magnitude, I've never been good at disguising my feelings – she always seems to know when something's up. I think – wrongly, as it turns out – that I've had the time to work out in my head what I'll say as I slide into the passenger seat; I've decided I'll be nice and calm, tell her what's happened, stay upbeat and conclude, *It's fine, it'll be OK, we'll treat it and get to the bottom of it.*

That's the idea. And sure, I try, but almost as soon as I

begin to speak, I fail hideously. Saying it out loud – 'It's a tumour' – to my wife of thirteen years, the mother of my children, the person who has been there for everything, from the highs of my greatest moments on the track and the births of our children to the harder times, makes it somehow completely real. In an instant, I'm breaking down, sitting there beside her in the car. The misguided notion that I would be able to hold it together sufficiently to get into the house to tell her quickly evaporates into snot and tears. Sarra is the one who flicks into practical mode. 'Whatever it is, we'll deal with it,' she says quietly, calmly. 'Let's get home and we'll talk about it.'

The day passes with me staring blankly at my phone while Sarra googles things and suggests we call our GP for advice. I am convinced it must be cancer because I saw the look of sadness and helplessness in the eyes of the shoulder specialist. That, as far as I am concerned in this moment, is that. I have cancer. I can't get further. Sarra, however, is insistent that cancer can't be diagnosed simply by looking and keeps telling me not to jump to conclusions and to wait. But I know, I just *know*, that a cancer diagnosis will account for all the niggles and pains I've been feeling the past few weeks.

That night, we try to be as normal as we can. It's the usual night-time routine for our children, Callum and Chloe: bath, story and bed. Now's not the time to mention anything to them, but children are incredibly perceptive, able to pick up any nuance of emotion. I'm holding it together, just, and we act as though nothing has happened. Life carries on as normal

– it has to, irrespective of the prognosis and what, unbeknown to me until a few hours ago, is going on inside my body. We stumble through the kids' bedtime numbly. When Sarra and I – both stunned by the day's events – finally go to bed, we just hold each other through the night, talk about everything, and cry. Even in this state of shock and fear, I feel awful I'm going to have to put her through this. What 'this' is, I don't know, but it feels sinister and I remain convinced there's only one answer. Will I need my shoulder amputated? Am I riddled with cancer? Every twinge sets off a mental reaction, and my body is tired and fizzing with adrenaline, so there are a lot of them. Is it already head to toe? I've no idea. I'm terrified.

The next day, I'm scheduled to be speaking at an event in London. Part of me doesn't want to go; the other part wants my mind occupied and is glad of a way to mute the spiralling fear, even if only for brief moments. I've mastered putting on a bold front – usually at a velodrome in peak competition – but this particular iteration, after last night with the kids, is much harder to handle. Before I drive away, I can see Sarra is worried and unsure that going is the right idea. She talks me out of listening to any music, anything emotional – *just a funny podcast*, she suggests. She's right, and in fact I'm oblivious to what I eventually pick. Whatever it is that plays out is no more than a muffled noise as I head down the motorway, a background to the intermittent calls that come in, about the next steps and arranging the next appointment. I survive the day, managing a brave face at the event. The journey home and the night that follows are much the same as before: concentrating on the kids and focusing on the mundane routine while we wait.

Looking back on those early days, some of it's a total blur, some of it so vivid. At points, it feels like I'm caught in a slow-motion spiral; at others, like time is racing away as appointments are booked in and my new reality starts to come into focus. I am suddenly a cog in a fast-moving machine as medical professionals work swiftly to confirm a diagnosis, which only heightens the sense of urgency about my situation. It is all-consuming. The next appointment is arranged for the following day, starting with seeing an oncological surgeon, who immediately arranges a second scan. Having endured one, in some ways I feel ready for the second, fuller scan and Sarra and I both hope it will answer our many questions and our uncertainty over the prognosis.

For the first scan – the one that changed everything – Sarra didn't come with me. It didn't seem important enough for me to need her by my side. After all, that was merely going to be a diagnosis of tendonitis. It would have been ludicrous to suggest I needed company for something so run-of-the-mill!

The second time, however, she is of course with me, along with the sense of foreboding and dread. Bar the London trip on the second day, Sarra and I are constantly at each other's side those first few days and weeks. I'm so thankful for that.

This time the scan takes ages, much longer than before. There's one particular area they keep revisiting – *that can't be good*, I think. A brief phone call is made in hushed tones,

I don't know who to – the doctor, I guess, to discuss what they've seen. My mind is swirling with possibilities and panic. Afterwards, I'm scared and upset, and searching the faces of the medical staff to see if I can read any cues about the severity of what's going on. Sarra holds my hand tightly, and I know she is feeling it too.

Later, when we're back at home, I get a call saying the doctor would like to see us in person. Instinctively, that feels like bad news, but when I ask, the receptionist reassures me that the hospital in question is on the doctor's commute home and he's the sort of practitioner who simply prefers to see his patients in person. I'm unconvinced, and we both brace ourselves for something bad, but the receptionist's reasoning is sufficient to get us through the day of waiting.

On arrival, we find the waiting room is dark, empty and silent as it's after normal hours, and I am relieved. I don't want to have to make small talk with anyone right now, and I want to keep this out of the public eye for as long as possible.

The wait seems like an eternity, and I'm using all manner of things to distract myself and persuade my mind that it'll all turn out OK. My finger hovers over the Wordle and Quordle apps on my phone, games I play every day when I have a few minutes and want to keep my mind turning over. Today, they take on a different significance: I'm staring at the games intently, thinking, *If I can solve this before they call me in, everything will be OK.* That's how desperate I am for good news; I'm resorting to childish superstition, not wanting to step on cracks, to conjure an illusion of control over what is

9

about to happen. I can't look at the apps now; I've had to delete them from my phone, the moment still so raw, the emotions of it flooding back each time I replay it in my head.

Sarra and I sit in nervous silence, I'm sure both having the same thoughts, and I'm still glued to my phone (I don't manage to solve the puzzle) when they finally call us in. As we shuffle into the consulting room, we are introduced to a nurse at the doctor's side, just like before. With her presence comes the sinking realisation that the news is unlikely to be good. Her demeanour and that of the doctor make me think, *Oh fuck, there's worse to come.* We sit down, side by side, holding hands, and brace ourselves for the impending news. Just like the first time, there's no beating around the bush. The doctor gets straight to it, saying, 'It's not good news. It's your prostate.' And in that moment I know it means it has spread. It means my shoulder is a secondary cancer. It has metastasised into my bones. My life starts crashing down around me.

I lean forward and put my head in my hands. I am lost. The doctor tells me that it has spread to my bones in multiple areas. Shoulder. Pelvis. Hip. Spine. Rib. He says 'I'm afraid it's incurable.'

And just like that, in a doctor's office after hours, I learn how I will die. I'm utterly helpless to respond. How will I tell the kids?

My brain starts going through all the things I've taken for granted that I'd be there for, that I was going to do. I think how I – all of us, really – take good health for granted. I have always worked so hard to remain fit and well, but with that one devastating sentence, as 'health' disappears from my grasp, I realise how lucky I was to have it. I don't start to cry, I don't have any reaction either on or below the surface, I'm just completely numb. I go green in the face, Sarra tells me afterwards. I definitely feel nauseous, I can't form words or even thoughts to ask any questions, but I am vaguely aware of Sarra doing that while I sit there. The noise is distant, the words totally indiscernible.

Throughout my career, both on the track and when I stepped away from it, I've always had a plan and a goal. I work towards things, applying and tweaking as I go, with an end in mind. I reach for targets with optimism and determination. No matter what happens, there's a way to get through it. On the day of the diagnosis, it feels like everything I know or understand about how life works has been ripped away from me.

I'm at a loss.

I feel hot. I feel claustrophobic. I think I'm going to be sick. I rise from my chair and squat down on the floor. I'm holding on to the ground, too stunned at this stage for the tears to come even though I now feel the emotion building – which is why, I suppose, I got up, as sitting was too much to bear. I glance over and see tears in Sarra's eyes. I'm trying to control my breathing and fighting the urge to run out of the room and away from this devastation that has suddenly become my life.

Prostate cancer? I was too young for this, I had had no

symptoms whatsoever that would point to cancer, to this sort of cancer. This just didn't make sense, how could this have happened to me? I have led a clean, healthy life, I'm still at the peak of my fitness, eating well, I've never smoked, never done drugs, and yet somehow these words were directed at me.

The doctor explains there was nothing I could have done – by the time I felt any symptoms (the shoulder pain being the first) it was too late, as it had already spread. Cancer is indiscriminate and in my case, living the healthiest of lives could not have prevented the genetic predisposition I have to it.

The nurse is introduced – Emma, who is a Macmillan nurse. A Macmillan nurse? This confirms the dreadful gravity of the situation. And then there's another doctor in the room, who introduces himself as the consultant surgeon. I'm finally able to find my voice and I ask what stage it is. 'Stage 4,' comes his reply and I think, *But that's the most severe stage.* Sarra asks about treatment, but they correct her and call it management. As the information keeps coming, and our new reality is laid bare, I'm not quite having a panic attack but I'm struggling to breathe. I somehow summon the courage to ask how long I have. It's a completely surreal question to ask. The surgeon informs us the prognosis is two to four years. It's like being hit over the head repeatedly during the course of a half-hour conversation, like being kicked when you're down and then kicked and kicked again. Sarra has her arm around me now. 'I'm here, it's going to be OK, whatever happens we're doing this together,' she tells me.

My breathing is laboured. Has it got to my lungs? My head hurts. My brain too? In that moment, death feels imminent, as though it will come overnight. There's no sense of how two to four years truly looks, the possibilities it could contain. The nurse gives us her card and tells us we're doing brilliantly. I appreciate the sentiment, but I feel like I'm failing as much as my body is. I hate to think what doing badly at this looks like; I spent the appointment green in the face, holding onto the floor, mostly in a squat, struggling to breathe. If that's good, then what's bad?

Just before we leave, we stand in front of the hospital's automatic doors, briefly pause as they slowly open, and go through what feels like a gateway to a terrifying new world, where we are already completely new people. We walk in silence like ghosts to the car, parked just opposite on the road, holding hands but absolutely, completely, utterly empty and bereft. Nothing will be the same again.

I don't remember anything about the journey home, the familiar sights and sounds we pass as we head back. I'm mostly thinking about the kids: Callum, who's nine, and Chloe, who's six, waiting for us at home and being looked after by a friend. I tell myself I have to snap out of it for their sake, urge myself to find a secure footing. I can't let my expression betray me so, like before, we need to get our game faces on. We park outside, gather ourselves and, without needing to discuss it, we tacitly agree to make it just like any other night with the bedtime routine. Now's not the time to tell them: we need to know what my treatment will be, and we need more time to deliver the news calmly, but even with that decision made for now, the idea of ever telling them weighs heavier than everything else.

We'd explained to our friend, Nina, that I had a medical appointment for a bad shoulder and asked her to stay up with the kids, said there was no need to put them to bed as we wouldn't be long. Coming home, we both know we will have to converse with someone for the first time since the diagnosis. I have no idea if we are going to say anything to her or not. Part of me wants to scream from the rooftops, and part of me wants to never breathe a word out loud to anyone, to pretend it isn't happening.

We turn the key in the lock, open the door and click into our usual cheery mode, get the kids occupied with something. As Nina is leaving, she asks if everything is OK and I tell her, saying it out loud for the first time: 'I have Stage 4 cancer.' Her mouth falls open in shock. She gives me a big hug and I'm a bit tearful as she releases me. I bathe the kids, read them a story, we have some laughs. It's hard, it's beyond hard, but it's also the reassuring rhythm of daily life. Both of us are disguising a wobbly chin, but we get through it. As I'm upstairs with the kids, a Sainsbury's delivery arrives. I can hear Sarra doing the small talk with the delivery guy, then there's food all over the kitchen surfaces. To all intents and purposes, we go through the motions of what should have been a normal family weeknight – only it is anything but. We feel numb and detached from reality.

The next person we tell, after the kids are in bed and the shopping has been put away, is Sarra's sister, Rachel. She's the medical director of the Marie Curie Hospice in Edinburgh and an expert in palliative care. I never thought that her professional life would cross with mine. She offers to drop everything and come down to see us. Sarra normally swats away such offers of help but, in an instant, accepts, unable to make any other decisions. Rachel agrees to come down from Edinburgh first thing in the morning to accompany me to the onslaught of medical appointments that await me.

What follows is the longest night, full of tears and panic, and this total sense of a fear of the unknown. We don't sleep much, fitful snippets at best. Every now and then, I'm hit by this sudden gust, like a pounding on my chest, forcing me out of bed, gasping for breath. I know it's terrifying for Sarra to witness but there's nothing I can do to stop it. She's quick to reel me back in each time. 'You're here,' she says. 'We're here, we're OK. The kids are OK. They are sleeping soundly next door. This might be happening but it's not happening right now, it might be coming but it's NOT HERE YET. Look at me, you're fine. You're not drowning, you have to swim, kick, breathe and get to the surface.' Each time, she quickly gets me back and, amid it all, I'm so, so appreciative to have her in my life, grounding me, getting me through.

Daylight and the morning come as a relief, like those long, lonely nights when the children were small babies and unable to settle, and the sunrise offers respite from the darkness. Right on cue, Callum and Chloe burst into the room, jumping onto the bed. They already know Daddy's got a sore shoulder so they're gentle, acutely aware something's wrong but blissfully unaware of the catastrophe we now find ourselves in. Twelve hours on from the worst news imaginable, we take selfies of our four smiling faces because we don't know how many more mornings we might have. Worry, fear, uncertainty bubble just below the surface, ready to engulf me.

We drop the kids at school on the way to the Christie, Manchester's cancer hospital. How has it suddenly come to us heading to this place, somewhere I never imagined myself forty-eight hours ago? The pace is dizzying. I sit in the car as Sarra takes the kids in and I call my sister, Carrie. I hadn't intended to tell her but as soon as I hear her voice, I crumble. It's a horrible phone call for both of us. I realise telling people this news requires more thought than I am capable of right now, more answers than I have. I'm in tears by the time Sarra makes her way back to the car.

As we drive to the Christie, conversation turns to logistics and the need to tell our parents. They live close to each other in Edinburgh and we initially consider driving there the next day to tell them in person. It feels the right thing to do. My father, who has had prostate cancer of his own to contend with, is a full-time carer for my mum who has Alzheimer's. The one positive in all this is that my mum won't be able to understand and grasp what's wrong with her son. However, after another conversation with Carrie, and another with Rachel, they do the telling. In retrospect, it is the best decision we could have made. When I do get the chance to speak to my dad, he is simply incredible, showing me so much strength. He tells me there's no need to drive up to Edinburgh to see them, to stay put and do what I need to do at home. Sarra's parents are the same but even her dad, usually so stoic, is in tears on the phone as they offer to drop everything to come down.

I'm grateful for the outpouring of love from my family and from Sarra's. That day, my mind keeps casting back to my friend Richard Moore. Richard and I used to cycle together when we were much younger; he was co-host of the excellent *Cycling Podcast*, author of loads of sporting books, a respected journalist and, more than all this, a really good friend. He'd died suddenly at home at the age of forty-nine, just eighteen months previously. What he would have given for another night with his wife, Virginie, and their son, Maxime, even to be able to say a proper goodbye. He didn't get that opportunity. I think about him and his family a lot in those first few days. I think too of Rab Wardell, a former mountain bike rider and another all-round lovely guy, who died suddenly in his sleep a few months later. Whatever my fate, I have the chance Richard and Rab were both denied – to say goodbye to loved ones. If this is the way it's going to go, I'll have to make the best of it. There's no other option. But how?

That Friday, the day after the diagnosis, is tough. At the Christie, bloods are taken and the medical treatment starts with an injection. I know it's life-saving stuff but it doesn't feel like it is saving me or prolonging my life. Instead it feels like the first nail in my coffin. I can't see much hope right now. I'm still trying to compute everything that's happened. This time yesterday, I didn't know, I didn't know what was coming for me. But now, just hours later, I am looking at the end of my life. My death is hurtling towards me. Some might say it's like an out-of-control rollercoaster – but at least with a rollercoaster, there are some fun bits along the way. This is more like a slow-motion car crash: painfully slow and clearly catastrophic, and no one can save me from it. I'm alone, tumbling to the finishing line I never want to reach. Quite how soon, I've no idea. It's nightmarish.

By now, Rachel has arrived and is here to help guide us. Given her job and her expertise, I know she might have the answers to some of my biggest questions, but I'm too scared to verbalise them. She treads carefully, giving me gentle pieces of information and advice when I am brave enough to ask for it.

Most importantly, she helps us navigate telling the children and suggests we tell no one else at the moment, until we have made a plan how best to tell the kids. Protecting them is our absolute priority. As I realise the reality that we will have to explain my situation to them, waves of uncontrollable emotion come – shock, fear, horror and grief.

Those first few nights see the greatest volume of tears. I cry more during them than I have over the rest of my lifetime combined. We seem to take turns spiralling out of control: me one moment, Sarra the next as the waves of grief engulf us, while the other seems to find the strength to cope. That's one of the reasons we're so compatible: we're able to haul each other out of such pits of despair.

In the early weeks, some nights sleep won't come; others, the exhaustion of it all kicks in and we're both knocked out cold. Each morning is the same, waking to feel OK for just a fraction of a second before the dawning realisation of this death sentence hits.

I think a lot about the time span in those first few days. Two to four years is just twenty-four to forty-eight months. Every week seems important, every day even, and with each one that passes, I'm closer to my end: how will I get myself in a place where I know how I want to spend them? That weekend, Chloe happens to ask Sarra how old she'll be when I turn fifty, just a passing comment by a kid working out numbers. But it stops me in my tracks: it's three years away. Will I even make it that far? And then follows the realisation that the prognosis means I won't be around to see the kids finishing primary school. Down and down I go, on a spiral of things I'll miss, things I'll never know and always assumed I'd get to do. I know I have to take control of my thoughts but this feels impossible right now. Sarra tells me that's the only thing that's hurting us – thoughts – and she's right, but it's hard not to let such thinking patterns creep in.

In those first few days, I try to cling on to normality wherever possible. It's just about surviving and putting on a brave face for the kids. I don't know if they sense anything is wrong. I don't think so. That weekend we take them to their BMX classes at the National Cycling Centre, next to the Manchester Velodrome. Walking in the same entrance I did countless times in my career, it feels so poignant to enter the building this weekend, with our children. A place with framed pictures of me and quotes of mine painted on the walls, all reminders of some of the highest points of my career, my life. These reminders poke at me, as if to highlight how quickly things have fallen apart.

As a kid, I loved BMX so much, bitten by the bug after watching the Steven Spielberg film *E.T.*, and I've never really been off my bike since then. I don't know if my kids are quite as obsessed as I was at their age but they're having fun, there are lots of smiles, I'm taking pictures, filming them, even commentating their imaginary races as they pedal along. Every picture and video we take feels significant and important, like I'm documenting my last time with them. Death feels within touching distance; I am still caught in a purgatory between knowing things are bad but not how much worse they will get, or how quickly. Thoughts, thoughts, thoughts. Sarra is right: they're what's hurting right now, and I don't know how to get a handle on them.

I am so raw that weekend that there are moments when I just utterly crumble, but what I begin to discover is that some emotional waves of despair are fleeting and they don't necessarily last long. I can break down while making a cup of coffee but then a minute later be sitting happily in front of *The Simpsons* with the kids, laughing away.

Monday comes around before I know it and I am back at

the hospital, meeting my oncologist for the first time. Sarra and Rachel come with me. Rachel is able to take notes of the important details and ask questions, which allows Sarra simply to be with me rather than having to cope with the admin side of it all too. Having someone else there is unbelievably helpful for both of us. The doctor suggests we shouldn't look at my scans as they will only frighten us, and that is helpful advice but also only adds to the terror.

Over the first few weeks, I feel lost, as though I'm living in a world of which I'm already no longer part. We're fully into autumn now, the leaves starting to fall and the days getting shorter and darker. A lot of my time in bed in the dead of night is spent awake, listening to the wind blowing and the rain falling. It's the nightmares I remember from those first few days and weeks, as my mind attempts to process the trauma of it all. Every morning starts with a panicked wake-up or the blissful naivety of the first blinking of the eyes – either way, it rushes in each time, that sinking news. It's my goldfish moment, going around in this same awful cycle. My brain is taking time to get used to the fact that I'm dying *now*; it's no longer this abstract concept we all have to deal with at some point. It's coming at me, and it's coming a lot sooner than I thought. Sarra keeps telling me, 'This isn't a conversation for now, we're not there yet,' and she's absolutely right, but I can't help thinking it. Thoughts, thoughts, thoughts.

I'm not entirely sure why, but I buy a thousand-piece jigsaw from Amazon in those first days of the various diagnoses and medical appointments. It's a landscape of mountains, water and boats, and it gives me something else to focus on. I'm not sure what makes me go for a jigsaw, it's not something I've ever really entertained, either as a child or in adult life. But it's a constant that's there for me, something almost stable, and it half helps. I say to myself, *one more piece and another and another*, and the time passes, without emotion. Concentration briefly blocks out the dark thoughts that pervade. It's maybe the only semblance of slight order in my chaotic world.

CHAPTER TWO

2012–13

Until the day of the diagnosis, I'd always felt lucky, certainly exceeding the expectations of that kid on the BMX bike who just wanted to be Elliott from *E.T.* Now, I feel lost, an observer looking into the world I am no longer part of. I know somewhere in me are my resilience and my fight, but I am going to need a lot of help to find them again.

Even the end of my cycling career went better than I could possibly have hoped. Not every athlete gets to choose how they bow out, but mine was the perfect finale – in a film, it might have come across as a predictable Hollywood ending. In my final race, in front of my home crowd, at my home Olympics, I held off the world's best sprinters to win keirin Olympic gold and become the first British athlete in history to win six Olympic golds.

Even twelve years on, I can instantly bring back the feelings and emotions from that day, simply by closing my eyes – the energy, the euphoria, that wall of sound from the crowd following me round, almost pushing me to the line. I'll never tire of reliving it.

The keirin originated in Japan after World War Two, created

as a gambling sport to help boost the nation's economy. The event is inherently unpredictable and difficult to control as a rider, or to predict a winner as a fan. To the uninitiated, it's a surreal sight as six riders battle for position behind someone setting the initial pace riding a derny – basically, a small motorised bike – who then peels off, allowing the cyclists to battle it out over a three-lap sprint to the line.

It wasn't my original event: that was the 1000 metre time trial, in which I won gold at the Athens Olympics in 2004. In 2005 we were informed this event had been removed from the programme for Beijing 2008. I wasn't ready to give up on my Olympic dreams quite yet, so I took on the challenge and in the end participated in the team sprint, keirin and individual sprint, winning all three. I became the first British person in one hundred years to win three golds in one Olympic Games. After Beijing, then aged thirty-two, there was a suggestion from coaches within the team that I should consider retiring before London, to accept that my best days were behind me as I would be thirty-six at the Games, an age at which no one had ever won a medal in a sprint event before. I disagreed, believing I still had a chance of being competitive. I wanted to go out there and give it my best shot. If I didn't win, I'd smile and wave to the crowd and bow out. I just knew I couldn't give up on the chance of experiencing a home Games.

There were a lot of challenges heading into London 2012 – injuries, crashes, defeats, public expectation of success and not to mention my teammate Jason Kenny, the new wonder kid of British sprinting, who was setting the world alight. He'd already shown what an amazing talent he was in Beijing, but he had really blossomed in the intervening four years and challenged me for the single places going in the sprint and keirin events. As the triple Olympic champion from 2008, everywhere I went I felt like I had a target on my back; in the keirin, I'd always taken it on from the front and now my rivals had got wise to this and were doing everything they could to try to stop me. So, I had to learn new tactics and become more versatile in order to outwit my rivals. The public expectations were sky high, but nothing compared to the pressure I was putting on myself and my desire to win gold again at my final Olympics.

The team psychologist, Steve Peters (more about him later), taught me, amongst many other strategies, the 'helicopter technique' – a coping mechanism to help deal with pressure and gain perspective in your life. In essence, the aim is to visualise the situation causing you stress and imagine yourself rising up above it in a helicopter, going higher and higher, all the while looking down on the problem. The higher you go, the smaller the problem becomes as you look out and see how tiny and insignificant you are in comparison to the wider world around you. The purpose of the exercise for me was to find perspective and realise this was not life or death and the world would not stop revolving if I didn't win a bike race. I came to the realisation I was riding a bike around a wooden bowl in anticlockwise circles. My job wasn't saving lives or curing disease! By gaining this new frame of reference I freed myself from the burden of pressure and instead looked upon this situation as a once-in-a-lifetime opportunity.

Curiously, on the eve of the London Games and at a time when I was relying heavily on this analogy to keep calm as my nerves started to rise, I found myself flying into London in a helicopter in order to carry the flag at the opening ceremony. Until that moment, I had been in my own bubble, focusing on my training and preparation, shut off from the wider world at our holding camp in Wales. I remember landing on the outskirts of London and being driven into the Olympic Village to be greeted by a massive block of flats with my picture all over it, maybe stretching up twenty storeys high. Far from feeling small and inconsequential, there was my giant image staring back at me. How was I supposed to imagine a helicopter high up enough from that? I recall thinking *This is absolutely ridiculous*, like something straight out of the movies. I'd come from relative obscurity, competing in a minority sport for most of my career, to suddenly being one of the faces of the Games. It was not going to be a straightforward task to keep my head screwed on for the next two weeks. The challenge was to focus on the process of what I had to do, both on and off the track, at every moment of the day: training, rest, diet, planning distractions to make sure I didn't find myself thinking about my rivals, what they were doing or even the outcome of the race itself. I didn't think about winning or losing, I simply focused on what I had to do to get to that start line in the best shape possible to give myself the best chance of winning.

On the day of the keirin I knew I couldn't control everything and, no matter what happened in those next few seconds, my aim was simply to try to enjoy the experience, knowing that a calm and positive mindset would allow me to perform at my very best. In the minutes leading up to the final I reflected on all I'd done over the past weeks, months and years, my whole career leading to this point. I reminded myself I could not have done more. I had truly given 100 per cent in every effort of every session, both on and off the bike, pushing myself to the limit each day, even when there were no crowds to cheer me on and when no one was watching. The drive had always come from within. I was ready to show the world what I could do.

There's nothing quite like that moment in any race when you make the decisive move. You always have a plan going in, but you also have to rely on your instincts to judge the perfect moment to launch your attack. That explosion of energy as you commit with everything you've got: that is your one shot. With this physical effort comes the response from the crowd the instant they see the move. It's almost as if the harder you press on the pedals, the louder it gets inside the velodrome. The sensation of surging around that final bend, hunting down the finish and then lunging for it, throwing the bike over the line to gain those extra few centimetres of reach and that last split second as you realise your wheel is ahead of everybody else's. There's the briefest of silence as the crowd registers the result and then there's that noise again. The roar. You finally look up and you see all those ecstatic faces looking at you, on their feet, screaming for you, caught up in the shared delight of that one single action. I've never experienced anything like those few minutes in the aftermath of the keirin at London 2012. I was riding around, at one point with my head in my hands, the next arms in the air, fists pumping, waving to the crowd, picking up a Union Jack, relishing every second. The rush only lasted a few minutes but even now I can still clutch at snippets of those memories and feel it again.

The keirin was my sixth and final gold medal and marked the end of my Olympic career, but in fact we had got the ball rolling on the first day of the track competition with victory in the team sprint, earning me my fifth Olympic gold. For a relatively controllable event, with none of the unpredictability of the keirin, it was still a hugely nerve-wracking experience. With Phil Hindes leading off and Jason Kenny completing the second lap, I would be bringing it home with the anchor leg, doing all three laps.

Expectations were high coming in as defending Olympic champions, however Beijing was the last time we had actually won a team sprint at World level and the French had been dominant in the intervening four-year period. We had struggled to find a replacement for Jamie Staff, our lead-out man in 2008, and having tried lots of different combinations with different riders in the squad, the trio came together only a matter of months before the 2012 Olympics.

We managed to break the world record heading into a final against the current World Champions, France. I felt huge pressure and responsibility doing the final lap and bringing the team home. Basically, I had to chase Phil and Jason over the first two laps as they were going flat out, whilst conserving as much energy as I could to keep in reserve for the final lap. The tension on the start line as the crowd hushes and the countdown beeps begin is like nothing else. I still get a Pavlovian response when I hear them now, with lurches in my stomach and adrenaline spikes. The feeling of responsibility that comes from being in a team and knowing that you don't want to let your teammates down. You know how much you have all put in to get to this point and you want to ride for each other, but the fear of being the one to make a mistake and cause everyone the disappointment of missing out is overwhelming.

The gap between the semi-final and the final was only about 40 minutes and I remember the cool down from the semi-final morphing into the warm up for the final and feeling like I hadn't had a chance to catch my breath. But as I sat on the start line on the gold medal ride I tried not to think too far ahead and instead simply focus on the here and the now: come out of the start line with every ounce of energy I had. My priority was to get on to Jason's back wheel. I treated it like a standing quarter laps we did in training, nothing more. The race didn't exist beyond that first quarter. Once I reached the quarter lap mark, I extended that mental side to the end of lap one, never allowing myself to think beyond the present moment. And then before I knew it, I could hear the bell and Jason was peeling off and leaving me alone. I don't remember much about that final lap, simply battling through the searing, stinging pain in my legs and the burning in my lungs, knowing it would soon be over and sensing we were up on the French from the sound of the crowd. I could sense that victory was within our grasp.

Paul McCartney, Kobe Bryant, the Royals amongst many others were all there to see our team win; the velodrome was the hot ticket that day. To get the ball rolling and be the first team to get a gold medal was the best possible start to our campaign and would signal to our rivals that any hope of our gold rush from Beijing coming to an end was in vain.

There was genuine positivity everywhere. People would tell me later exactly what this was like and how it felt as if the Olympics had united the country, giving people an escape from their everyday stresses and a reason to talk to one another. I have been told even strangers began to strike up conversations on the Tube, feeling part of it all. People were so proud of their athletes, it was just the most wonderful couple of weeks that ended perfectly for me. As athletes, being part of the class of 2012 with people like Jess Ennis-Hill, Mo Farah, Andy Murray, Ben Ainslie and Kath Grainger, we were acutely aware of how special this was and we were grateful that our careers had coincided with this precious moment in British sporting history.

Having said that, the enormity of London 2012 was amplified by the fact I knew it was my last Games and that I had the chance to become the most successful British Olympian of all time in front of a home crowd. No big deal! As much as I publicly played it all down, saying I wasn't thinking about it, of course I *was*, but I was trying to use it at the appropriate time. It wasn't right to think about it on the start line of a race, but I used it as an incentive and motivation in those days, weeks and months of training to bring out the very best in myself. I used to turn to it in the dark hours in the middle of winter when I was training, still eight, seven, six months away from the Games, when life felt pretty heavy going. I'd allow myself to daydream and would use it on a wet, dark, early Tuesday morning to get out of bed and into the gym, or when I was grinding out that last rep on the squat rack. I would think of Sir Steve Redgrave's remarkable five gold medals and push on and imagine how amazing it would be to potentially have my name mentioned alongside Sir Steve's, a long-time hero of mine.

The build-up to 2012, my fourth Olympics, was like no other, and so was the aftermath. After Athens, I had returned to my flat in Salford to sour milk and bills to pay, and aside from a few exciting events, life returned to normal very quickly. But Beijing was the game-changer – I wasn't ready for the sort of reaction that followed. The combination of Britain having its most successful games in a modern era, finishing third on the overall medal table, plus me being the most successful member of the team meant that everywhere I went people seemed to know me. It was a huge change in my life, particularly as I have never craved the spotlight. By London I was becoming used to being recognised most places on and off my bike, and the bizarre reality that people knew me and might do strange things like grab my thighs in public, uninvited!

I thought it couldn't possibly get any more intense, but I was wrong. From the moment of carrying the flag, through to becoming 'Britain's greatest Olympian', things shifted . . . markedly. After leaving the velodrome after my second gold, I remember pulling up alongside a police van – they spotted me and so I lifted up my medals to acknowledge them. Their van door slid open and out they got to stop the traffic and pose for photographs with me. There was a sense that everyone was sharing in the collective euphoria and it was magical.

The day of the Closing Ceremony, the medallists were invited to Team GB House in the heart of London where we spent an afternoon sitting and chatting with Hollywood stars like Sylvester Stallone, Jean-Claude Van Damme and Jason Statham. All the while, on stage, Tony Hadley was singing Spandau Ballet's classic hit 'Gold' to a room full of Team GB gold medallists and we all sang along for the chorus. I just seemed to flit from one surreal moment to the next and somehow it all seemed perfectly normal at the time. From then on for the next few years my name found its way onto the invitation list for all sorts of spectacular events such as presenting at the

Film Awards, presenting a BAFTA, winning an NTA, winning a GQ award, hobnobbing with Kylie Minogue backstage before giving an acceptance speech on behalf of the Olympic team in front of Bono, Noel Gallagher and many others. Streets, velodromes, marathons, road gritters and llamas were named after me. I was given the Freedom of the City in Edinburgh which included being offered a free bus pass for life!

Briefly, people treated me like some sort of proper celebrity. If I stopped anywhere for a moment, I'd be mobbed. Going anywhere in public was difficult, especially in those first few weeks. I remember walking out on stage at Hyde Park, wearing a tracksuit with my medals around my neck. I wasn't performing, singing, doing anything bar waving, and I felt like a rock star amid this frenzy of excitement and interest. People could remember sixteen years before at the Atlanta Olympics where Britain had won just one gold medal. This time we had them coming out of our ears. And for once people didn't need to be a fan of cycling or athletics or swimming but simply whatever Britain was doing well at . . . which was quite a lot, as it turned out.

It was madness, pure and utter madness. For those first few weeks, I often needed to be escorted by security or police to get me in and out of venues. I can't remember how many trains I have missed at Euston because it was impossible to get through the crowds by myself to catch my train due to the number of selfies I was asked for. I remember Sarra posting a picture on Facebook of us together, me with my medals around my neck, and the caption *I've got him back*. She hadn't really though, because instead of finding any down time after the Games, I was booked for events from breakfast until the dead of night. Each day felt like a week's worth of work! I was run ragged and exhausted but it was so much fun and I wanted to make the most of it as I knew it wouldn't last forever.

At times, I was embarrassed by the attention, almost a bit self-conscious. I love praise, like anyone, but after a while it became too much. I didn't like to be recognised whenever we went out, to have people always looking at me. We'd walk into a restaurant and I'd often hear my name being whispered around the room. People would whisper to their friends, who would stop eating and turn to stare. It felt so uncomfortable. I don't think that in the first sixty or seventy days I ever slept in the same bed for more than two nights as I hopped from one thing to another, from a seat on a chat show sofa to doing the loop the loop in the co-pilot seat of a Eurofighter jet, all these amazing experiences. I knew that in six months I'd probably be old news, so it was a case of embracing every single bonkers experience, even if I was longing for my own bed and a bit of good old-fashioned routine and normality.

By December 2012, it was decided that the best chance I had of returning to normality and the training routine I was by then craving was to head to Perth, Australia, our familiar winter training base for over ten years. It was arranged with a view to getting out to start training again and still in that post-Olympic haze, as a special dispensation, we were allowed to bring our wives and girlfriends. (I chose to take my wife, wink.) I slowly got back into the training but, as luck would have it, I got sick and ended up in hospital with days of diarrhoea, vomiting and horrendous stomach pain that simply wouldn't dissipate. At one low point, I was directed into the hospital bathroom with a container to provide a sample. It was like trying to use a pressure washer to fill an eggcup. As you might imagine, it didn't end well and I sheepishly handed the sample to the nurse whilst apologising profusely. Thankfully, whatever it was eventually passed – they never found out what it was – and I was discharged. But I was totally wiped out by the experience. A decision was made by the coaching staff that there was no point in pushing my body and I was advised to just do light training and use the time to let my body recover. It felt like a real breather, a moment to pause and take stock.

For so long, I had focused solely on London and I couldn't look at anything beyond that point. It had been such a challenge just to get there in one piece. Life didn't exist past London, this single date looming in the calendar and, after it, blank space. And then in the madness of what followed, I never quite had a moment to think about it either.

Perth was my much-needed opportunity to return to a training block and work out what would come next. My thinking was *let's see how it goes*, with an eye on the potential of one final hurrah – a proper shot at the Commonwealth Games taking place in Glasgow in 2014. The opportunity of a second home Games was a massive deal for me, especially as I had never competed in a major event in Scotland. But it was becoming apparent with illness and injury that my body was waving a white flag. I'd already pushed myself to the limit and I didn't feel that I wanted to continue at a level that was below my previous best.

I think what eventually swayed it was I realised I was content and completely satisfied with all I had achieved in cycling. I didn't feel the need to pursue any more cycling goals. With that realisation came the understanding that there were many other opportunities and things I hadn't yet tried. I began to look forward to a more balanced life pursuing lots of different things instead of one, at the expense of all others. The most significant of all that was starting a family.

When making the huge decision to retire from their sport, no athlete really knows for sure if they're making the right call. It's not uncommon for elite athletes to make a u-turn and come back for one last go, but ultimately I was so fortunate that it didn't feel that way for me. I began to see the Glasgow Commonwealth Games in a different light: as an event I could immerse myself in, be part of as an ambassador and enjoy from an entirely different perspective. Reframing it in this way allowed me to see it as a whole new exciting opportunity rather than dwelling on something that had come to an end.

I knew which way the decision was heading, but it was a trip Sarra and I took that made me certain. In 2013, we went on a massive eight-week trip to Cambodia, Thailand and then Australia. I've always loved Australia but had never gone much beyond the environs of some of its main cities: Melbourne, Sydney and Perth, for training and competition. I had a deal with Jaguar at the time and they kindly lent us a car to use for the road trip. We went everywhere, from Brisbane all the way up the Sunshine Coast, clocking thousands of miles in total, with a roof rack and our bikes on the top of it so I could ride as I saw fit and get some training under my belt – cycling part of the route from Melbourne to Adelaide, for example. From city tours, to exploring the beaches and shark diving, we tried it all, including the wine. I'd never done wine tours before and had our first in the Barossa Valley. I remember having a first wine tasting at nine o'clock one morning and thinking how weird that was. By ten o'clock, it didn't feel so weird and by lunchtime we were flying!

At the end of that marathon road trip, all there was left to do was return the car to the dealership in Brisbane. We were just half a kilometre away and I thought we should do the right thing and get the car cleaned so we could return it in a respectable state. I drove into the car wash, forgetting the two bikes on the roof. Just as Sarra asked, 'Are you sure the bikes will . . .', there was suddenly an awful crunch overhead. Having driven thousands of miles, I'd come unstuck within the last mile! The top of the tunnel had caught the bikes, and a bit like opening up the roof with a tin opener, had ripped the roof rack tracks from the car, bending the A pillars, cracking the windscreen but remarkably leaving the bikes relatively unscathed. The bikes were some of the first prototypes for my own brand of bikes and I suppose the only good thing to come out of this episode was we could truly say they had been tested to destruction.

When we came back after such a remarkable trip, I'd just turned thirty-seven and knew the time was right. I was ready to retire. Like with all these things, somehow news had leaked out and I flew back straight to Edinburgh from our trip and then headed to Murrayfield Stadium for a press conference. As I stood behind the door before coming out, I couldn't shake the feeling that if I stayed there and didn't come out then it was not officially over. It was one of those funny tricks the brain can play at life's biggest moments, the good and the bad ones.

I thought I was handling it well, but then the music started playing as I walked in. I had a montage play-out that the BBC had kindly put together for me. It hit me. I realised I was going to get emotional, and there was a great big lump in my throat.

I sat down, said thanks for coming and then, 'I'm here to announce my retirement from track cycling'. Again, in a flash before I said it, the words got stuck in my throat and I thought, *until I say the words I'm not retired*. But in that one short sentence it was over. It all felt very final. I was done. I'd known for a good couple of months that this was my decision but being able finally to voice it publicly felt like a big relief. It was a big, wide world out there and there were other things

I wanted to do. I was so grateful for the career I'd had for so long and loved for so long. To imagine as a kid that one day I would be able to make a career out of riding my bike would have been ridiculous to suggest, unthinkable even. And I'd not just scraped by but achieved infinitely more than I ever thought was possible. I'd wrung out every last drop, and I was done. What joy and satisfaction it had brought me, the places it took me, the people I met and the lessons I learned had set me up for life.

In the days afterwards, one question kept going round and round my head. For eighteen years I had defined myself as a professional cyclist. What was I now? I remember going through immigration at Miami airport shortly after retirement and filling out the visa form. It asked for my job title. I had no idea what to write. It felt as liberating as it did terrifying.

CHAPTER THREE

2023

IN my career, I've always had a plan, a target. There's always been a finite point to aim for. With this diagnosis, the end point is absolutely the thing I want to avoid. How can I plan for it? I certainly can't aim for it. In that early awfulness I can't even begin to strategise or consider a way to tackle it. My life has been stopped in its tracks, as my future becomes obsolete and my usual optimism evaporates. I stop laughing, and I stop whistling. I even stop making the bed, the small daily acts that happen unconsciously when I am happy.

It's stifling. I think, *There isn't a way out*, and the days are dark, very dark, and very long.

But without realising it, I have instinctively already begun building a group around me. There's Sarra, obviously, then her sister, Rachel, so quick to come down and join us in those impossible early days. Our close immediate families surround us with love and care despite their distance from us. My old team psychologist, Steve Peters, always used to talk about building a troop around yourself when training for big races and how that troop and their opinions are the only ones that matter. He taught me how to tune out the noise of everyone else. He's been invaluable to my career and has become a friend and pretty quickly I know I will be able to lean on him to help me negotiate this tough road ahead.

When I first met Steve in 2003 I was already a World Champion and Olympic silver medalist, but I had none of my Olympic gold medals. I knew that was my ultimate ambition, and when offered the chance to meet with this new addition to our team, a psychologist no less, I jumped at the chance. I was eager to work on any aspect of my racing and training that could be improved. Before meeting Steve, I was the sort of athlete who often rode emotionally. If I was feeling good on the day of a big competition, I was difficult to beat, but I could be easily distracted and sometimes swayed by the environment around me.

Steve helped me change all that and refine how I approached the mental side of my performance. It's quite remarkable to consider that being an elite athlete isn't simply about the physical exertion; just as I trained my body in the gym, he made me realise training my mind was vital in order to achieve my true potential. And, in the same way that you don't get strong after one session of lifting weights, there's no quick fix to becoming mentally strong; it takes time and it takes consistent effort.

He enabled me to develop a toolbox to deal with pressure situations and understand the futility of focusing on things I simply couldn't control. It was all about 'controlling the controllables' and the importance of concentrating on the process rather than the outcome. His philosophy is based on the 'Chimp Model', in which different parts of the brain battle to dominate. That emotional, 'fight or flight' response, which at times I'd had difficulties keeping control of in the heat of competition, is the 'chimp'. Steve taught me how to address the fears and emotions of the chimp with logic, thereby eradicating negative thinking patterns or behaviours. He was also so good at breaking down what I was doing and helping me step back to see the bigger picture. At the time, to me, track cycling seemed like it was the most important thing in the world – and it was – but he'd remind me and other riders, with a smile on his face, that all we were really doing was riding around in anticlockwise circles. It was our passion and of course it mattered to us, but it wasn't life or death. When viewed like that, it became a lot easier to put the tough results into perspective. He kept me level. That approach was a key factor in my first Olympic gold in Athens, and his advice was just as crucial in London eight years later. With his help, I was able to go into that immense pressure cooker that was the Lee Valley Velodrome and think: *This is just a bike race and if I don't win, I'll ride around the track, wave to the crowd with a smile on my face and life will just go on. And I'll still have five Olympic golds!* With my worst-case scenario being reframed as a smile and a wave, I freed myself of the burden of expectation, rode around in anticlockwise circles and won the race.

Steve's input didn't just improve my performance on the track, he also had an immense impact on my life off the bike, helping me use those same tools to translate into everyday life and how to approach everyday situations. He helped me to recognise who I wanted to be and how I wanted to live my life, how to tackle challenging moments and do it all with a positive outlook. When my cycling career was over, even though we could go months without seeing each other, our paths would still cross occasionally and Steve always welcomed me as a friend. This meant I would often find myself turning to him for advice at different points, including during my motorsport career that followed. Thanks to the work Steve did with me for all those years in the team, ever since then I have felt better equipped to deal with the curve balls that life can throw at you.

As a close friend and confidant, Steve is actually one of those first people I tell following the diagnosis. He is shocked but manages to conceal it well. He later admits that the news had thrown him and brought him to tears. In the early days of diagnosis, when the doom and gloom are flooding us and my negative thoughts are overwhelming, I know I need Steve's help more than ever before.

I need Steve's help for my own mental state, to try to talk me through this, to help me get back to functioning again. I need him to stop me going down a terrible Google rabbit hole after the consultations. I am worried about Sarra who has the burden of caring for me, dealing with all of the admin a cancer diagnosis brings whilst putting on a brave face for the children, supporting them through a big transition as they themselves have only just started at a new school. I want to be able to find my strength again, for her.

There are so many new things to consider when you get hit with a cancer diagnosis. No one can prepare you for the shock of it, but also you can't fathom the sheer volume of paperwork you're presented with. I find myself incapable of dealing with any of the admin; seeing the severity of my diagnosis laid bare in black and white on a printed sheet of paper paralyses me every time I see it and so Sarra takes it all on. The amount of paperwork and phone calls is huge and I'm struck by just how fortunate I am to have someone as amazing as her by my side during all of this. To navigate all this alone must be almost impossible.

So, after a few phone calls, I drive to see Steve. On the way there, I realise my first question for him is really big, but also very simple: how, in the face of this diagnosis, do I go on? How do I make the best of this? After all of our conversations over the years about keeping things in perspective, suddenly it really is life or death! How do I keep myself able to function on a daily basis, put one foot in front of the other, crack on, look after the kids, just live a normal life? That is what I want with the time I have left.

Steve lives in a beautiful place in the middle of nowhere, down a long driveway and complete with a donkey sanctuary. He greets me with a hug and he is so calm, putting aside twenty years of working together and the friendship that has come with that. He hides any sign of his own upset he may feel. He focuses on questions, mixing the personal with the medical: when did I get diagnosed, how was I, what did the scans show, to get the full picture. Steve's approach has always been to go with the flow of whatever life hits us with, and this is no different. It is immediately comforting to me: this is big, yes, but there is still that same grounding approach that has helped me so much in the past.

We both sit down and out it comes. He lets me unload, listening to the thoughts that have kept me awake most nights or locked in deep, strange, nightmarish sleep. He reassures me I'm not going to be dead in four or five weeks, helping me see for the first time that none of the doctors has ever mentioned weeks, but in fact they have been saying years. The fear that death was imminent was my chimp panicking, it was my unfounded fear. It's the first time I can really hear that, and the next step is to learn how to begin to envision what those years might hold.

Steve also helps me understand that a lot of the feelings I have are simply grief. Grief for what feels like a life lost. Gaining some insight into this terrible feeling helps me begin to process it. Before I leave that first meeting with him, he asks me what I've understood, and to play the conversation back. In repeating the crux of our conversation back to him, I'm worried about myself, Sarra, the kids, and of course I feel vulnerable, but already I feel that little bit better. I've been able to face some of these fears head-on and Steve helped me examine each one slowly and provide a rational explanation for each one. Saying them aloud to someone who didn't try to dismiss them but instead encouraged me to examine them has helped and finally relieved a bit of pressure in my head. Incremental improvements are all that matter at this point.

For a day or two after this first meeting I feel light, but then inevitably, like a game of snakes and ladders, I fall back to square one and without warning suddenly feel just as bad again. On the bad days, when in a pit of despair again, I find it hard to reach out, even to Steve, with my chimp telling me there is no point. I begin to realise I need to plan ahead and try to speak to Steve regularly, even when I feel OK, because when it comes, I am currently unable to outrun the fear.

So in those early days, I speak to Steve quite a lot to express what I feel and to deal with the emotional side but also the practicalities. I've always liked a plan and for that plan to be fact-based, and I begin to see that I can approach this next stage of life in the same way. Racing bikes around velodromes and dealing with cancer might not be relatable on the surface, but the approach to both is actually similar. It's about having a plan, reviewing it and constantly managing it.

Outrunning a terminal illness is a lot tougher than going for Olympic gold but ultimately it is about a person facing challenges and finding ways to take them on. One of the hardest to conquer is pain. I'm in pain right now from the tumours that are affecting the different parts of my body and I'm afraid of how bad this pain will eventually become. Steve explains, reassures almost, that this pain will subside, that the drugs and treatment will shrink the tumours and I'll eventually get to a point of being pain free. And with that, the twinges that have caused me huge anxiety since the diagnosis, every one feeling like a new tumour, a new threat, a new step closer to death, become more manageable to cope with. This deeper understanding helps me see this as a condition to be monitored and observed but not feared.

Steve comes to an early appointment with us at the Christie so I can introduce him to my oncologist, there by my side to piece through all the medical information but also to ask the pertinent questions. Similar to Rachel who has returned to her family in Edinburgh, Steve isn't there to treat me but to help me navigate obstacles outside of the appointment. I can't bear to ask the most difficult questions of my oncologist for fear of the answers, but I find that I can ask Steve. He helps me find the hope in what the doctors – always so careful not to give false hope – are saying.

While all I can see is still this damning diagnosis, its finality, both Sarra and Steve are more upbeat. Sarra hangs onto the words 'years and years' and keeps repeating them to me. I can't really hear it from her because it feels like she is clutching at straws for my sake, but it is Steve's response after each appointment or blood test, when he talks about the future, that begins to give me a firm foundation. Gradually, I am better able to see that there will be more of a future than I thought. One of his foundational messages is looking at 'years ahead'. While it all still feels imminent to me, weeks not years, I am finding it easier to listen to him, to see further ahead.

Throughout it all, Steve is also doing some background reading and research, answering the questions I am too afraid to verbalise, and comes back to me with stories of what he has read. He talks about the statistics around my diagnosis, how they're rough but not quite as bleak as the headline statistics I can find on Google. He explains that the statistics about prognosis are already outdated, based on old data. He also shows me how there's been a real surge of interest in prostate cancer in the last four or five years, there are a lot of new therapies in the process and lots of different safety nets. The hope is that science is moving faster than my cancer. This is hope laced with realism, and it feels good and gives me courage.

He finds examples of people in the UK and around the wider world in the same situation as me who were given a similar timeframe but have lived ten, fifteen years longer than the average cancer patient in the same position. I'm not naive enough to think there's some miracle cure out there, but anyone going through Stage 4 knows the thing you need above all else is hope. This information has planted some seeds of hope and I can feel the hope is beginning to grow. And along with that hope, suddenly other shoots of light start to appear.

These shoots of light can come from the strangest of places. Sarra's friend Sam, whom she was with when I had that first scan, and her husband John both know about my diagnosis. They have been an invaluable support to us both, especially in these early days. Sam has since done some reading of her own and stumbled across Andy Taylor, the guitarist of Duran Duran. Sam carefully sends the article to Sarra, saying 'it may not be the right time to read it right now but anything that may give some hope'. Back in 2018, Andy was given a very similar diagnosis to me – Stage 4 prostate cancer – and in 2023 had been deemed suitable for palliative, end-of-life care. But having been offered a new type of treatment he's now asymptomatic and the indications are he has a good few years ahead of him, which wasn't the case when he was first diagnosed. The article Sam sends about him is too raw for me to read in that moment, but I simply forward it to Steve to delve deeper into. His message when he's been through it all is simple: 'I think this might be worth looking at.'

This seems like something that might genuinely help: here is someone with my diagnosis. I really want to talk to him.

I liked Duran Duran growing up and was lucky enough to sit next to Simon Le Bon once at a dinner at Goodwood House, when I was there for a motor racing event. Often when you're there for the evening you've no idea who'll turn up for dinner: leading businessmen and women in their field, sports stars, Hollywood A-listers, musicians, it could be anyone, and I got talking to Simon one night. Little did I know how different my next encounter with Duran Duran would be.

My manager, Rob Woodhouse, tracks down a number for Andy's manager and after a few days we speak on the phone. I feel like a drowning person desperately clutching at any sort of life raft that'll give me positivity and keep me above the surface. I just need to hang on, to talk to someone who's gone through a similar situation to mine and get an understanding of what that experience was like. I know it must be difficult for him to relive what it was like for him and when he heard the words 'Stage 4' for the first time; to remember how he felt, how he reacted, the next steps and the forming of a plan to battle it. But he is generous and frank with me, and I'll always be grateful for that. He tells me just how he felt when he received the diagnosis and how he felt his life had ended. It is exactly how I feel; it's the first time someone has truly struck a chord with the challenge facing me and what is swirling around in my head in these early weeks. During our conversation, he could not be more of a force for positive change if he tried. He's fought his way back from end-of-life care and found extra time on this planet, for which he is eternally grateful. Following that chat on the phone, he's kind enough to send messages to ask me how I'm getting on. Andy is my shining light and his attitude gives me hope and lifts my spirits, giving me an insight as to what might be possible.

He also tells me about the treatment he had, a treatment we hadn't been aware of until he mentioned it. His saviour, as it were, was Professor Chris Evans, someone Andy calls 'the Elon Musk of cancer', who was responsible for administering him Lutetium-177, a type of radioactive treatment that targets cancer cells and effectively makes him radioactive for a few days in the aftermath. As Andy put it, 'Chris Evans gave me my life back,' and enabled Andy to relive his life again. Andy agrees to introduce me to the Prof, as he is known.

Chris has been knighted for his services to the medical world and is one of the leaders not just in cutting-edge cancer treatment but in biotechnology. I hadn't been searching for a cure in those early days and weeks, I knew that simply wasn't possible. But with Steve's help, I realise that what I was looking for was someone to say there's hope and there are options, and I will do whatever it takes to get you to live as long as possible. And I think I might have found the person.

Up to that point, no one had been saying this and it felt like that was missing. On paper, what I have – what countless people have – is a catastrophic result, but there are people living long periods of time with this and actually doing really well. Having the contact details of Prof Evans, who readily agrees to talk to me, feels like I'm doing something proactive to start fighting back. It's not much but it's a start. It feels like Chris might be the person who can offer me hope on the medical/scientific side. I first speak to him on the phone, and he is just what I need. Immediately, he is the polar opposite to anyone I've spoken to.

The Prof is completely different in his approach. During that first call, Chris is full of energy and exuberance for life: he has hope and wants me to focus on that. I find myself hanging on his every word. He isn't giving away anything confidential but is able to reel off case studies of other people and how he has helped them. The message coming back to me over that speaker phone is that he can't promise anything, but that there are people responding well to treatment and they are still going. He offers ideas and bits of practical advice, things to do and not to do, things to keep me moving forward. He is a new person to add to my troop with his own skills to add to the mix.

The language he uses is totally different from that of the other oncologists too, and it's almost disconcerting at first. His messages usually begin with 'alright boyo' and his sign-offs more often than not instruct me to 'stay cool'. It's not the solemn delivery I've come to expect and I can't help but warm to him and smile. It releases another bit of pressure. 'Stay cool.' I don't need Steve to translate this: there's no ringing in my ears, I find myself present and able to listen and take in what he says. After a few more exchanged messages, we go down to London to see him in person.

Although hope is beginning to emerge in fits and starts, I'm still not in a good place. That week, I have an appointment in Manchester that reveals the tumours growing on my spine are dangerously close to my spinal cord. I am issued with a list of dos and don'ts and when to call for immediate medical assistance. My anxiety around every twinge in my body is back, and despite all Steve's help I am finding it hard to see beyond the next few months, unable to plan or truly hope for it.

There becomes an urgency to certain things and we take the chance to make a trip to London to fulfil a bucket-list moment. Among Sarra's and my many plans for the future, we had always spoken about one day going to see the Chemical

Brothers play at Fuji Rock Festival. The Chemical Brothers have been the soundtrack not just to my cycling career but to my life in general. I am a huge fan, and when I ended up meeting Tom Rowlands randomly at a cycling event a couple of years ago, I struggled to contain my excitement and I cringe now at how much of a fanboy I was! Funnily enough, he has a passion for cycling, so we became friends over the weekend and he said if I ever wanted tickets for a show just to let him know.

With the unspoken understanding that we may never get to Japan now, we discover the Chemical Brothers are playing in London that same weekend, and he very kindly arranges tickets for us and some of our closest friends to watch their gig. I am struggling to be positive because suddenly it feels like a 'make a wish foundation' bucket-list gift, where our friends have downed tools to be there with us, at this farewell gig, the last I'll see. Sarra however is quick to correct me, telling me it's not the last but instead the first Chemical Brothers gig we will have been to as a married couple. 'There will be plenty more,' she keeps saying. 'It's going to be really embarrassing when you're still here in ten years' time when you told everyone you're dying!' She is firmly clinging to any optimism she can, and I'm grateful for that.

I chose standing-only tickets, wanting to be right in the heart of the action, but as it is just days after being told about the state of my spine, how brittle it is and the dangers of it being knocked or damaged, I'm feeling slightly vulnerable. I can sense Sarra's worried, wanting to put a protective ring around me as we go forward with the crowd. It's absolutely fine and I'm just trying to be grateful to be there at this truly mind-blowing show, but I still feel vulnerable, knowing a sudden shove can have catastrophic consequences. Our friends with us know about the diagnosis and are doing their best to remain upbeat for my sake, amidst their shock. But they don't know this latest news about the tumours on my spine, the time doesn't feel right, and this makes me feel more isolated too. I can't bring myself to be fully in the moment and I start to spiral: if this is the last time I'm at a gig, why can't I be fully present? It is an emotionally charged evening, during which I hold it together until the middle of the night, when lying in bed, the grief overwhelms me once again.

Later that month, we go to see the Prof. His office doesn't have that hospital environment feel but instead is an ultra-modern open-plan office space with staff working at their desks, an amazing team of specialists in different fields of cancer, using their expertise to find ways to help people, improve their lives and find treatment or even a cure for all types of cancer at different stages.

At the end of the large swanky room is the Prof's own glass-fronted office, facing everyone else's. His office is far from what I am expecting. It is completely incongruous with the modern office environment. It's like Albus Dumbledore's, lined with shelves full of all sorts of mad and magical things all over the place. The first thing that catches my eye is that his place of work is covered in memorabilia from Welsh rugby, and you can't miss his Welsh accent from growing up in Port

Talbot. There are also guitars all over the place. As I later find out, he's an amazing guitarist and a big fan of Led Zeppelin and Pink Floyd. He has all manner of video and audio clips of him at various events, having got on stage with some of the biggest rock stars in the world to raise money for the fight against cancer. It's surreal, as mid-appointment he slides out his phone to play one particular clip of him performing 'Stairway to Heaven' with Led Zeppelin to me, Sarra and another doctor who's joined us.

Charlie Chaplin once said, 'Life is a tragedy when seen in close-up but comedy in long shot.' In that moment, it seems very apt. The other doctor looks like he's seen this all before and even though we're here to talk about my cancer, I'm happy for this slightly alternative approach. With each glance around the room and with every new minute of this meeting, I like Chris more and more. He is just so full of energy, in his mid-sixties, not that you'd know it, and it's an energy that is truly infectious. He makes me feel like I have to get him on my team. While there's an overriding atmosphere of positivity in the room, I'm still emotional and struggling. At one point, Chris says, 'I'm sixty-six next week. When you're back here on your sixty-sixth birthday . . .' and he leaves the thought hanging in the air. I'm tearful because that seems such a life extension to what has been said before, but I also feel, frankly, that even sixty-six is no age to die. The flickers of hope are still just flickers: I can't yet see a way to come through this.

The Prof is not involved in my care or treatment plan and he reassures me that the treatment I have been offered at the

Christie is exactly where I should be and is all perfect. This I had never doubted for a moment, but what I also know is that it is inevitable this treatment will at some point run its course because cancer is clever and adaptable. We get some blood tests and Chris explains various other modes of treatment that might be available to me when the treatment I'm receiving at the moment – the chemotherapy and cancer drugs – stops working. I don't remember how long the meeting lasts, but it feels like it's all over in a flash.

Chris is not involved in my cancer treatment for now, but he has offered himself as a sounding board and source of additional advice as and when I run out of other options. Knowing that feels like a safety net has been cast out, catching me mid fall.

As I walk out after that first appointment, I don't exactly feel elated, but I am so buoyed by the chat, Sarra too. We walk across the street and bump into the television presenter Richard Hammond. He stops to say hi and I briefly feel compelled to tell him about my cancer and the meeting I've just had, but I think better of it. Instead, he suggests we should do some filming zipping around in cars and catch up. And I happily agree, realising that the idea of making plans for the future might actually become a reality, that my life might continue. It's been a bizarre morning but a good one, the first in a very long time.

Sometimes in these early days, I just want to rip off the plaster, to tell the whole world about my diagnosis, but I choose to refrain to allow myself, my family and friends time to let the shock of it all sink in. Being in the public eye puts you in the spotlight a little, and as I see more and more people, there are more and more ways the news can leak out despite us being careful not to let that happen. And that's where the other part of my team, alongside Steve Peters and Chris Evans, come in: my agents Rob, Sara and Lucy, who have done such an outstanding job of looking after me for nearly fifteen years now. They come to the house and reassure me that they will do all they can to protect me and keep my news quiet for as long as possible. But we know that if and when the news leaks, we should have a plan. Rob and I have always been about having a plan, that's why we've worked together so well for so long. So, with Rob's help, I put together a statement. Reading it back weeks later it's pretty bleak, but it's a reflection of how I felt at the time. We might not need to use this one, but at least we're ready to go with it if we do.

Rob's so good at listening to me, especially in those first days and weeks, talking about work commitments I might or might not be able to do. His message is that I can do as much or as little as I want and it's up to me, he'll just move with that. I like to keep busy the whole time – I always have – but I have no idea how I'm going to be in the coming weeks, once the chemo starts in particular.

In the initial few weeks, I find myself under pressure to seize every moment. It proves emotionally exhausting, as I try to impress upon the kids just how much I love them ('NO! I love YOU more!') and try to hold them in a hug whenever they stop moving. I catch myself even in the most mundane moments somewhat ridiculously thinking this is the best glass of water I've ever tasted or look at that amazing cloud/bird/ tree. I can't keep living with this intensity, it isn't sustainable.

There is a desire to document everything too, so I am taking endless photos and even though I have never been a diary keeper, I am attempting to write everything down. Now, reading back what I jotted down in those early days, it's a slightly rambling stream of consciousness. I also feel obligated to do something monumental, thinking I need to raise millions for charity, climb Mount Everest, swim the Channel or *something*. I also consider it's time to learn how to play the guitar. But I realise I can't worry about any of that right now, it's about enjoying the simple moments of each day. The ritual of a morning cup of coffee, watching a comedy show on TV, playing with my kids or even doing a track day in my car – I have to aim to simply be present.

As the days begin to tick by, suddenly the start of chemo looms and my thoughts turn (even more than usual) to the kids. I know we just have to tell them. I've always identified with the idea that you're only as happy as your unhappiest child, and I am hyper-aware that my news, when I can bring myself to tell them, will make us all very unhappy and may change their childhood forever. At the moment, they're oblivious, simply happy kids charging around the place. I watch them and my heart breaks thinking of what this news will do to them. It's something I am terrified to do but I realise we have to. In those early days, there was a danger the news would somehow get out and the kids could end up finding out in the school playground. This was even worse than the idea of telling them, but I can't envisage a time when I will be able to tell them the news without breaking down in the process. I know I'm going to have to be the strongest I've ever been when we do decide to tell them.

The biggest block for us is not knowing how they'll react. There are two ways to approach it: tell them in a public place, somewhere they won't necessarily have to return to so there'll be no recurrent association with the bad news, or tell them at home. In what feels like a heavy and sad conversation, Sarra and I decide we will tell them at the kitchen table, during normal dinner time, in the hope they won't have awful memories of being told to 'sit down, we have something to tell you'. Chloe has only recently turned six and doesn't know the difference between lunch and dinner time. To try to explain a timescale to her at this stage seems barbaric and torturous for both her and us, not to mention confusing, when we are hoping for so much more time! We want to take away as much uncertainty as we can and ensure they feel secure with the information we are about to give them. Sarra and I discuss the questions they are likely to ask and the answers we will give. We know they will be led by our reactions, so we both take a deep breath, smile and begin dinner.

I remember trying to make it sound as casual as possible, despite my stomach churning and my head full of thoughts and emotions. I am hovering in the kitchen and Sarra is sitting down with them. 'You know when Daddy went to the doctors,' Sarra starts and they both look up inquisitively. I then take over. I explain the doctors have found the cause of my sore shoulder at last. 'Have you heard of cancer?' Callum, quick as a flash, eyes widening, says 'yes', but Chloe looks a little more confused. I go on. 'Well, I have cancer in my shoulder, but the doctors have got medicine for me to try to fight it. The medicine is called chemotherapy.'

We make sure not to say it is a cure but simply that it is going to make Daddy feel a bit better. They are both looking straight at me, not taking their eyes off me. The first thing Callum asks is, 'Are you going to die?' It's not the stab in the heart you might expect, it is the response we prepared for, but even still, I am surprised at my ability to remain calm. We agreed to be honest and clear with the kids to the extent we could at this stage. 'None of us live forever,' I say. 'We all die at some point and no one knows when this will be. However, we hope that I'm going to be here for many, many years because of this medicine I have. Chemotherapy will help me feel so much better. It might make me feel unwell, look unwell, I might even be in bed, but it's important to remember that's not the cancer making me ill, it's the treatment that's pushing the cancer away.'

The kids are looking concerned and a little cautious so Sarra adds, smiling, 'Look at Daddy now. Does he look OK?'

'Yes, look at me, do I look all right?' I ask, and they slowly look me up and down as though to check for any weaknesses.

'Am I looking sad?' I add, smiling. They shake their heads and then I'm on my feet, putting Chloe over my shoulder as I gallop round the kitchen with her to prove my point. And then it's over, we're smiling and laughing together. I'm so relieved, exhaustedly so, and it's gone way better than in my wildest dreams, a scenario that has played out hundreds of times in my head already before this day. With Chloe giggling on my shoulders, a giant weight has been lifted off them.

Knowing that once chemo starts, I am not to venture too far from the hospital, or at least stay in UK territory, Sarra and I decide to go on a trip beforehand, just the two of us. With the support of her sister and parents, we are able to arrange five days away. And so, New York City joins the Chemical Brothers on the bucket list. I've never been before, it was always in my sights, but right now I have no idea if it is the last trip of this kind I'll ever be able to take, despite the optimism from Prof Chris and Steve. But again, Sarra and I try to think of it as a first, one of many firsts, a more positive way to approach this next, uncertain segment of my life.

New York is an amazing city, like nowhere else in the world. It's fast paced, busy, noisy, bustling, and I feel like a blur, caught in the middle of a time-lapse picture. We stay in a hotel slap bang in the middle of Manhattan at the start of the Christmas build-up period. Sarra's best friend Kelly lives in New York working for the UN. When she heard the news she dropped everything and flew straight home to be with Sarra and me, the sign of a deep friendship indeed. Kelly and her boyfriend Matt have cleared their schedule and make themselves available to us throughout our trip, showing us around and giving us space in equal measure. They are able to read us perfectly.

Each day Sarra and I would get up and walk and walk and walk some more, clocking up something in the region of eighty thousand steps. It creates headspace to think, and with chemo looming, there are some serious life considerations and conversations to have. But sometimes we're walking and I'm sent into an emotional spiral by a sight, sound or thought, and I duck into a doorway, pulling the baseball cap over my eyes, and break down, sobbing uncontrollably. It's a few days full of tears.

Walking to the point of exhaustion, with my back and hips hurting, we fall into bed, often crying through the night, as we continue to cope with the grief of it all, eventually falling asleep at some ungodly hour. It's terrible but cathartic too, almost like a final purge of the tears before the chemotherapy can begin. I'm fortunate that I've never been depressed in my life, but I begin to wonder if this is what I'm now feeling. It's hard to describe it: grief, shock, depression, maybe a combination, but it's the darkest I've ever felt and like there is still no way through it, no answer, no solution, nothing really to look forward to. I am barely holding it together those four nights away.

I find myself at the top of the Rockefeller Center and watching people having the time of their lives. I'm enjoying that moment, catching sight of the views I've seen countless times in the movies and American TV shows. Right now, I feel like I'm in my own terrible film and there are moments that are so, so hard to contend with. Everyone else's lives are moving on and I don't feel a part of it. Everyone's buzzing with the early Christmas spirit and I somehow feel like I'm not really even there; I'm no longer part of this world but just observing it.

At one point, Sarra and I sit down on a bench in Central Park in front of a baseball batting cage. It's not particularly picturesque and there's no one using it. We quickly, and almost accidentally, get into a really tough and upsetting conversation for the pair of us. It is an end-of-days conversation: notwithstanding what Prof Chris told us and the stats Steve armed us with, we both know the end game here and where I am heading. Sarra promises me 'I won't let you be in pain' and I am just unable to respond.

Yet amidst this overwhelming grief, there are moments of joy. Kelly and Matt take us to a stand up comedy gig and I laugh. I belly laugh despite having spent the previous night sobbing. As time passes on our return, I am able to recall all of the wonderful moments we had and New York seems more magical, but God it was hard. People would ask subsequently how it was and I'd say *amazing, what a city*, but if I really think about it, it was profoundly challenging with some very dark moments.

As the countdown to chemo begins, I manage to pull myself up and out a little: I know I'm not special or unique, and people all over the world are somehow managing to cope with their own hardships, whatever they may be. Unseen and unknown faces, but somehow we are all in it together.

Now we have told the kids, we want them to be part of this treatment journey throughout, in as positive a way as possible. Sarra comes up with a lovely idea to represent regrowth and the passage of time from Winter into Spring. She has had the kids paint a big tree with bare branches. It's a beautiful creation, the idea being they will stick a piece of blossom on it every day throughout the eighteen weeks of chemo. It's called Daddy's Tree and each blossom will mark a step closer to completing treatment. A blossom a day should take us to late March, when chemo is due to end and around the same time the cherry tree in the garden will bloom. I'm not sure who it helps more, me or the kids, but as we start to glue the blossoms on and my chemo begins in earnest, I start to see the possibilities ahead.

CHAPTER FOUR

2013–14

AMONG the jubilant faces staring back at me from the stands at the velodrome at London 2012 was my Uncle Derek. A warm-hearted and intelligent man with a hilarious sense of humour, he was an avid supporter of me during my sporting career. I had always imagined that once I hung up my wheels and retired from cycling, the two of us would share an occasional whisky while he tutored me on the finer details of Scottish folk music.

However, that was not to be, as Derek died in November 2012 aged just fifty-eight. To a certain degree I was shielded from his illness during the Games themselves by my dad (Derek's older brother) and the family, but it had become clear to everyone during that time that he wasn't well. Almost immediately after the Games, he was diagnosed with an aggressive brain tumour and it all then moved so horribly quickly, giving his wife, Christine, and their daughters, Jenny and Sarah, hardly any time to get used to the idea of what was happening. Within weeks, he was hospitalised, and he passed away at home with his family at his side soon after. As a close-knit family, we were all bereft at his sudden loss.

Uncle Derek had been an incredibly talented musician and played the fiddle in the band 'Jock Tamson's Bairns'. I remember, some years before, going to a music shop just off the Royal Mile in Edinburgh that specialised in Scottish folk music to pick up one of his CDs. As I came to pay, the guy behind the counter looked down at the name on my credit card then back up at me and started saying, almost incredulously, 'Are you . . . ?' It was just after the Athens Olympics and it had been happening quite a bit, so I was already half nodding, expecting him to follow with '. . . Chris Hoy?' – but instead he excitedly said, '. . . related to Derek Hoy?!' It filled me with such joy, and it summed up not only how well respected he was as a musician but also just how modest and understated he was with it. Derek's talent outshone most around him, but he was never boastful. He had the perfect nickname too: 'Happy'. And beyond all this, he was also a talented coder for the National Health Service and had been a nurse in his younger years. No one had a single bad word to say about him and his sudden passing, as the youngest of four in my dad's family, was a big shock to all of us. I thought of him a lot during the early days of my own diagnosis.

The following year, in 2013, my cousin Sarah, Derek's younger daughter, married her lifelong sweetheart, Fin. Inevitably, all our thoughts turned to how much Derek would have loved it – the whole family united for one big party. In Derek's absence, my dad gave Sarah away and delivered a lovely speech. Our hearts were broken by the loss of Derek, but this gathering was so full of love and happiness. The whole thing was so wholesome and epitomised everything we felt about the importance of family.

Sarra and I have both always been very family-orientated. We have been so lucky to have such close-knit families. But until Sarah's wedding, children hadn't really been an immediate thought for us. We had felt too young and carefree plus I'd always struggled with the idea of being a father while at the height of my career: pursuing Olympic medals entailed a self-centred drive that didn't sit well with the idea of parenthood for me. There are others who manage it with children and frankly I'm in awe of them. Sarra and I had always assumed we'd start a family one day, but until this moment, we had never made plans. As we sat together at this beautiful wedding, watching our families united in laughter and sharing this incredible joy together just a few months after Derek's untimely death, we agreed that a family was what we wanted.

Some time later, I came home from work and suggested we had a glass of wine. Sarra looked at me sheepishly and told me she wouldn't be joining me, as she was pregnant. I laughed and laughed with the joy of being told such news. Our journey to parenthood had begun, and it felt quite surreal. It was hard to imagine that I was going to be a dad, or that there was an actual baby on its way.

When Sarra's mother was pregnant with her and then with

her sister, she suffered with pre-eclampsia, and given there may be a genetic link, Sarra was quick to tell doctors about her mum's medical condition and asked if there might be a risk of it with her own pregnancy. But the medical staff were very relaxed about it, reassuring us everything was fine because 'that's your mother's medical history, not your own'. And really everything was fine, it was a straightforward pregnancy for the first two trimesters. Sarra was well, very active and waiting for a bump to show.

Looking back now, there were indicators, clear moments where things had started to change and become less than perfect, but we couldn't see that at the time. It began when Sarra was doing an overnight shift as a volunteer for the Samaritans. She had begun to feel very unwell with what felt like really bad heartburn and started vomiting. I wasn't overly concerned at all as she appeared to make a good recovery, and she reassured me she felt well. In fact, she recovered enough to attend the Pride of Britain Awards a few days later. A pain came back a little across her chest, but she put it down to being in a formal dress rather than her usual Lycra. We look back at the photos from the night and can see Sarra's face looks unusually puffy and swollen. We didn't see it at the time because bodies change so much during pregnancy, but now we know more, it is clear that it was actually an early indicator of pre-eclampsia. Like so many would-be first-time parents, we didn't have a clue. Only hindsight makes us realise just how naive we both were.

A few nights later, Sarra was struggling to settle and sleep, which was unusual for her, despite coming towards the end of her second trimester. She woke me early on in the night to tell me her heartburn had returned. I remember her politely but firmly sending me off to sleep in the spare room. 'You're not going to get to sleep in here if I'm up and down throughout the night, and you have a really busy week of work,' she said, so off I went.

An hour later, the door opened and sleepily I asked if she was feeling any better. In a rush, she told me she had resorted to calling 111, the NHS non-emergency number, to ask if she could take anything else for heartburn, but after spelling out her symptoms in that middle-of-the-night call, they had insisted on sending an ambulance. 'It's on its way!' she exclaimed in horror. 'What the . . . !?' was my initial reaction. 'I thought it was just heartburn?'

Within minutes, the paramedics arrived. I, meanwhile, was still trying to come to from a deep sleep. Sarra was so embarrassed that she had summoned paramedics to the door in the dead of night for a case of heartburn and was mortified when they insisted they would have to take her to hospital. Such was her discomfort about wasting NHS resources that she tried to talk them out of taking her – that very British reaction of 'everything's fine'. They became quite stern and reluctantly she agreed to go. She looked apologetically at me and tried to make light of it by whispering 'at least this will make a funny story'.

She later told me she was offered gas and air in the

ambulance for the pain. She laughed that off, saying, 'I think we can wait for the baby's arrival!' I followed behind in my car, not particularly concerned as I was following Sarra's lead. She had kept reassuring me this was simply heartburn, although she did admit to me some time later that she had in fact never suffered from heartburn before, so just assumed it was supposed to feel that bad.

We were both comforted by the idea she would be checked over by medical staff and reassured this was probably all just protocol. I knew it was going to be fine and predicted this would just be one of those sleepless nights; she would be given a stronger antacid tablet and we would be home in an hour or two. It was just part of the trials and tribulations of pregnancy and, like Sarra had said, we would laugh about it all in a day or two. But what did I know?

Sarra was given more antacids when she arrived at A&E and almost immediately the pain subsided. However, I gradually realised that they believed this to be more than heartburn due to the number of tests and questions being asked as medical staff tried to get to the bottom of what was going on. It was five in the morning by the time the doctor came in and Sarra immediately started to slip her trainers on as if to leave. She was so embarrassed to have caused a fuss over nothing and was looking relieved at the prospect of being discharged. The doctor looked at her slowly and suggested she sit back down as, with a clipboard in hand, he announced that her blood results had come back. 'It suggests you've had a heart attack,' he said, looking bemused and perplexed. My immediate thought was that they must have confused the blood results with those of someone else in A&E. We both sat there open-mouthed, the doctor asking if there was any pre-existing heart condition or any history of it. Sarra looked a bit stunned – there was no history of it in her family.

Sarra seemed OK and the initial tests showed there wasn't a problem with the baby, but she was now to be transferred to a cardiac ward in a different hospital for further tests. We started casting our minds back over the past week to see if there were indicators. She recalled a phone call to her dad when she was heading to her shift with the Samaritans and telling him, 'It feels like I'm having a heart attack'. It was a throwaway remark in the midst of a stressful day, but it felt more pertinent on reflection.

Still, the baby was moving around OK, the pain had subsided, and while Sarra was being transferred to a hospital a few miles away, I went home to pack her an overnight bag. She hadn't yet prepared the 'hospital bag' for the birth, so it was down to me to find the correct items for her. She was sending me sporadic text instructions in between her medical tests with statements like 'the big pants' and 'the comfy pyjamas'. The pressure was on as I rifled through laundry baskets and drawers (it turned out that the G-string I initially brought bore no resemblance to the pregnancy pants she had requested and was not appropriate!). I drove to the new hospital to settle her in and found her on the cardiac ward, in a private room because the majority of patients on that ward were elderly men. She seemed so out of place, sitting up in bed, still insisting she felt OK. We were introduced to a calm and gentle heart consultant who suggested Sarra could be suffering from a rare illness called HELLP syndrome, which was fatal for the mother unless the baby was delivered. One of the features of HELLP – a very serious form of pre-eclampsia, he told us – was that the mother can appear well. But still more tests were being carried out, no decisions were being made, and I didn't get the sense of any panic or rush. Sarra would be kept in for a few more days yet.

With that in mind, Sarra insisted I should carry on with my usual work commitments and come back later that day. I had an event in the Manchester velodrome and I assured Sarra that it could easily be cancelled, that anything could be cancelled, but we decided in the end I'd attend. Mid afternoon, when I was finally pulling out of the car park on the way to the hospital, the phone started ringing. It was Sarra's sister, relaying messages from Sarra. 'Where are you?' was the first question, immediately giving me a sense of unease. Rachel said, 'You need to get to Sarra. They say the baby's going to have to come out.' *How can this be?* I thought. *She's only just twenty-nine weeks pregnant. The baby can't come yet!*

Nothing could have prepared us for what was about to happen. Further tests that day had shown the placenta was beginning to fail and the baby – we didn't know at the time if it was a boy or a girl – needed to come out. We were going to become parents, today, and I felt nowhere near ready.

I parked the car as quickly as I could and ran, sprinting down the corridors to get to Sarra. I knew I had to be calm for her. She was alone when the doctors delivered the news to her and she had relayed it to her sister over text, too upset to speak. She was clearly terrified, but trying really hard to put on a brave face.

What we came to learn afterwards was that when they had finally undertaken a detailed scan of the baby, there had been some degree of panic on realising the placenta was failing and the baby was measuring far too small. The last time Sarra had been scanned was at twenty weeks. No one could tell us what had happened in that intervening time. All we knew was that Sarra was barely even showing, with no more than a slight bump; some people would not even have guessed she was pregnant at that point. I couldn't get my head around the fact there was even a baby in there. The idea of it being delivered this soon was terrifying.

While we still didn't have a definitive answer on the diagnosis, it was suspected to be HELLP syndrome and immediate delivery of the baby was required in order to save both their lives. This was so far away from where we had imagined we would be. We were now suddenly facing the immediate delivery of our baby, eleven weeks early. After some discussions with doctors (and begging and pleading from Sarra), it was agreed that they would rescan her in the morning. If nothing had improved, or indeed if things were worse, they would perform an emergency C-section.

I was making positive noises, trying to calm Sarra, who was distraught. We were both beyond scared about what the future had in store for us and for our baby. We lay on her hospital bed together, trying to process the news and what was about to happen. We hadn't even chosen a name but knew we had to decide on one before this baby was born, so that he or she would have an identity from the moment they entered the world. Our baby was in grave danger and no one could give us any assurances about what might happen. I know Sarra feared the worst; when choosing the name, she told me she was imagining what it would look like written on an order of service at a funeral. It was a dark time.

When I finally left the hospital with visiting hours long over, it was a lonely drive home. Sarra was used to being alone in the house without me during my career, be that two-, three-month training camps in Australia or other competitions around the world. But I was always used to having her at home in bed with me. I don't think I'd ever felt so alone.

There had been so many times in life where I felt like I had the Midas touch, that luck had followed me. Admittedly, there was a huge amount of hard work involved, but looking back on the Beijing Games, London 2012 too, it just seemed to be that everything went my way. Everything had been falling my way since 2008: in my career, in meeting and marrying Sarra, and in starting this new life out of competitive cycling. I felt so lucky and was very aware of how happy we were.

Perhaps our share of luck had run out and we were on the cusp of life changing forever. I tried to be as rational as I could but I knew there was a chance that the baby might not survive the next day's C-section or might face significant disabilities. On top of that I couldn't even begin to imagine what I would do if something happened to Sarra. I was terrified. I can only imagine what it must have been like for Sarra, or try to understand the position she was in mentally, physically and emotionally. I was trying desperately to be a positive and supportive partner, but it felt impossible. I went to bed that night knowing that the following day we faced a challenge of a magnitude we'd never encountered before and that I had to show strength and courage to carry us both – no, all three of us – through it.

After all the chaos and panic of the preceding day, the morning of Callum's birth was actually calm. I came in to see Sarra who managed to smile and whisper 'Let's Steve Peters our way through this and control the controllables!' and with that we were quietly taken for the scan, which confirmed things were continuing to deteriorate. We were then taken immediately to theatre, and in fact the emergency C-section was actually the most peaceful point of everything in those difficult weeks. As Sarra was leaned forward and prepped for surgery with injections, I held her hands and to keep her focus on me rather than the fear, I started talking her through all the holidays we'd been on – Miami, Australia, Thailand, Cambodia – and it seemed to help.

When the moment came and they pulled our baby out, there wasn't a sound or a cry, although I could see frail little arms and legs moving. The doctor gestured towards me to show me my baby and I saw this unbelievably small creature. A boy! Like so many premature babies, he looked like a tiny baby bird that had fallen from the nest with no feathers on it. There was just nothing to him. Later, we found out he weighed just two pounds two ounces, barely a kilogram, less than a bag of sugar. But he was here, my boy, and I felt a rush of love and pride. I turned to Sarra in delight and relief and told her, 'It's a boy! He's breathing!' The nurse asked me if we had a name and I proudly said 'Callum'.

I was still terrified and couldn't believe this tiny thing was our baby. I was a dad and even though I knew it might be only for a short time, it was an overwhelming feeling. He was checked, quickly whisked away into an incubator, and then rushed to the Neonatal Intensive Care Unit (NICU) to begin his fight to stay alive. They couldn't allow us to hold him even for a fraction of a second, although I had the honour of cutting the umbilical cord, which was very special. All Sarra could do was catch a glimpse of him in his incubator before they whisked him away. Sarra wasn't well after the birth and was taken back to critical care. She didn't meet Callum until over twenty-four hours later when she was well enough to be wheeled into the NICU. It would be another four long days before we were able to hold him for the first time.

You have a vision of how becoming a parent will be. You've received those joyous text messages from friends announcing a baby's birth, the weight and declaration that mum and baby are doing well. However, in our case, as neither was fine in that immediate aftermath, I couldn't reassure anyone else or feel a sense of celebration. I did message family and friends to let them know what had happened, but it felt hard to celebrate in those first few hours and days. We eventually put a message on social media too and we were met with swathes of support. Gradually, we could both see that it was a cause for celebration; this extraordinary wonder of life, almost physically impossible, was a living, breathing human and he was ours. It wasn't quite the blissful moment we had envisaged but that feeling was still magical because it felt like we were witnessing a miracle. Sarra and Callum had passed the first hurdle: they were both here.

Going into the Neonatal Unit to see Callum for the first time, I was struck by how dim the lighting was, with a low-level purple haze illuminating the incubators. The staff moved around the room smoothly and calmly, but there was frenetic energy and a feeling of stress that came from the stifling heat and constant noise. There were machines everywhere, with monitors humming and alarms buzzing, all doing their thing to keep these sick and tiny babies alive. Breathing equipment whirred and hissed while alarms beeped and bonged constantly, some with a reassuring peep and others with incessant warning tones. I was directed towards an incubator near the corner of the room, and there, in the centre of this Perspex box, lay our tiny baby, no clothes on, a blindfold covering his eyes, his mouth and nose hidden under what seemed to be a massively oversized breathing mask and the rest of his body a jumble of wires and tubes. When I was finally allowed to touch him through the incubator, his tiny, thin arms and legs starting flailing as though in a panic and I became even more acutely aware of how fragile and vulnerable he was. I was scared that even the softest of touches would rip his delicate, velveteen, almost translucent skin. But regardless of all the fear, looking at him, touching him and seeing his chest rise and fall as he managed to take a breath, I was consumed by love for him. Regardless of what might come, I was a father. My son was in front of me, breathing, wriggling from my touch, and in that moment I knew I would do anything to protect him.

Sarra had to remain in hospital for the rest of the week while she recovered, which meant I had to flit between hospital and home and that we were apart. Each day, I was able to leave the NICU and head to the comfort of home and find respite from the emotional impact of the clinical world in which we were now immersed. The mixture of emotions was over-whelming. Every time I drove to the hospital, I felt grim because I didn't want to go in and see our baby looking so desperately unwell; but then, conversely, I urgently wanted to be with him too. I wanted to celebrate Callum's birth, but I also felt like there was nothing to celebrate because we were living hour by hour to see if he would pull through. I felt guilty about that and guilty that I could escape to catch my breath and go home, unlike my wife and son; and as soon as I closed the door to home and was alone, I wanted to return to the hospital and my family. I was horribly torn and didn't feel right anywhere. At home, I felt like I should be in hospital; at times in hospital, I didn't want to be there, I didn't want my wife and child to be there, but I knew there was no choice.

I knew I needed to be strong for Sarra and strong for Callum and I had to get myself to a place where I could do this for them. The thing is, deep down, I believed he was going to die. We just didn't know what lay ahead so I was determined to appreciate every moment. I was a dad – no matter what happened, I was a dad. I got to look at our baby and talk to him. Then I got to hold him. I'd take all that, if that was all there was. I wanted to savour every moment.

Watching Callum struggle and fight for every breath, watching him in such discomfort with his tiny body covered in tubes, was so hard, but I also knew that every breath he took was making him stronger, more likely to take the next one. It was (it is still) such a privilege to watch him grow with every hour, and though each visit required battling the dread, every time I saw Callum I felt a surge of pride at how hard he was fighting. In those strange, hard times at home alone, it helped me to go to the gym and lift weights, push through and make myself stronger. The thought of Callum helped me get through those sessions. He inspired me and I hoped I was sending those vibes and that strength back to him. In return, each day at the hospital, I would watch the numbers intently on his monitors, measuring every single input and output from his tiny body. Sometimes there would be big leaps back, but outnumbered by the continued tiny steps forward.

Meanwhile, recovering from her surgery and illness, Sarra was also trying to express milk for Callum, something we hadn't even started thinking about – another parenting decision we had to make far more quickly than we anticipated. Breast milk can be so beneficial to premature babies and the medical staff were keen to remind us of this; however, a baby born at Callum's gestation is unable to suck – they have to be tube fed – which means breast milk has to be expressed by the mother and then fed to the baby every two to three hours.

I had not really considered how we would feed our baby before now, but I can tell you I had never considered breastfeeding might look like this! It is a huge task for any mother, but in Sarra's case, because Callum had come so early and all the trauma she had been through, it was almost impossible. She would text me from the hospital while I was at home with pictures of the 0.2ml of colostrum she had managed to express. She continued to try to express milk every two to three hours each day. She tried relentlessly with all manner of pumps, but it often felt like she was producing more tears than milk. It was heartbreaking and so incredibly hard to witness her pain and anguish. I felt I was failing as a father and a husband, helpless to extract us from this situation and do the one thing I should be doing: protecting them.

Sarra was finally discharged and coming home was particularly hard. The last time she had been at home, she was happily pregnant and life was normal. Now we had a baby, but the baby wasn't here. As we reached our front door, the contrast between how we had imagined coming home at the end of her pregnancy and what was actually happening was stark, enormous. Sarra told me she felt a huge sense of loss and grief wash over her, realising her pregnancy had ended and the baby left behind in the hospital, and might yet die. There was a lot of fear of what might happen in the future. All I could do was try my hardest to support Sarra.

Each day, we'd go back into the hospital, timing journeys in between expressing milk and feeding times. We didn't know how long Callum would yet remain in the NICU and the doctors would never promise anything but suggested we would know more in a few weeks. Generally, babies might come home around their actual due date. That was another ten weeks away and so began our daily routine of spending every day at the hospital with Callum, and each night at home, without him. Each journey into the hospital we had to navigate through the darkest, wettest and most miserable weather. As the Cheshire rain fell relentlessly upon us, it perfectly reflected our dread and fear. Even now when I go down that road towards the hospital, I remember the dark ominous rain and that sense of not knowing what was to come.

As a couple, you feel so isolated in such an alien environment. Friends and family can do little to ease the pain and you cannot possibly imagine anyone could have experienced anything like this anguish that you now feel. You don't realise there's a whole world of other people in exactly the same situation. In fact it is far from an uncommon experience – just rarely talked about.

Still, in the midst of all this, we were reminded every day of just how lucky we were. After about ten days, the doctors told us that Callum had surprised them all and despite their initial concerns, they described him as a fighter and very strong. The overall suggestion was that he was now stable and in pretty good shape. But pretty good shape for a very premature baby is still unimaginable. I remember us walking in at one point when he was receiving treatment on his eyes. He was making a sound like no other – his helpless squeal will stay with me forever, it was awful. To be separated from your baby, unable to hold them or comfort them, was painful for me and excruciating for Sarra. We were quickly informed we shouldn't be there and they rapidly ushered us both out. Again, I felt so helpless that there was nothing I could do.

But from then on, I found my voice to help Callum. I knew I couldn't have much impact on the big medical stuff, but I was going to make damned sure every other part of Callum's care was spot on. Marginal gains and all that! So I would happily hush nurses if they were speaking too loudly in the intensive care ward, or question the doctors when I wasn't happy with his oxygen saturation levels. It isn't easy to find your voice in situations like that, when the natural instinct is to defer to authority, but part of this was me being Callum's dad. This was my role now.

As the weeks dragged on, we became more and more desperate to get Callum home. Having a baby in neonatal care does a funny thing to the concept of time, pushing and pulling it like a sci-fi movie. In the beginning we would have done anything to slow time down, to prevent Callum from being born so soon, so early, but the minutes, hours and days ran through our hands like water. And then once settled in the NICU, you want time to go faster but we found that it suddenly slowed to half speed, as if we were moving through treacle. It was almost painful. We were so desperate to get Callum home that when the moment came, it was dizzying. It seemed the doctors had been telling us for so very long that it was too soon to discharge him, and then suddenly they talked about his going home – tomorrow! I remember thinking, *Are you sure, why now?* We'd been waiting for so long and suddenly it was upon us and I felt completely unprepared.

He was still a couple of weeks from the original due date, he was still tiny, he had some issues with his chest and once discharged we'd no longer have round-the-clock care from professionals – it would be down to us! I didn't know if Callum was really ready, and I didn't know if I was either. Not to mention the fact we hadn't bought anything yet! Plans had been thrown into disarray and we hadn't considered the practicalities of if and when he finally came home. It had seemed too much to hope for. You would think we would've had plenty of time to make arrangements, but life in neonatal isn't quite like that: it is lived hour to hour and day to day. It really demonstrates to me just how much we had been living from one day to the next, not quite being able to imagine Callum coming home. So, we found ourselves racing to the shops to buy a car seat and a cot with just hours to spare, typically last minute for me, but definitely not the approach I had wanted for parenthood.

Leaving the hospital with Callum, now weighing a whopping four pounds, was a significant moment. I thought I would feel free and elated to leave the hot, stressful neonatal ward; I hadn't anticipated the apprehension and fear that began to bubble up inside. Driving him and Sarra home – a journey I'd done countless times in the grey darkness of winter, longing for them to be with me – I felt very tentative.

I'm told this is very common for neonatal families, but those first few days (and weeks to be honest) were a battle. Whilst thrilled to be at home with our baby, we were away from the familiar comfort and security of the hospital; the weight of responsibility began to loom large. There was just constant anxiety about Callum. He still struggled with his breathing, which was laboured, and he was at a higher risk of infection. Feeding and ensuring he was gaining weight was a monumental challenge. Being discharged didn't mean his neonatal journey was over by any means, and he was often so ill with bronchial issues that he was required to be hospitalised for a few days quite regularly.

We may have adapted to it, but it still wasn't easy. Sarra told me how she often feared the worst and each time she went into his room she would be making a plan for how best to call the emergency services, always preparing for the worst possible outcome. Thankfully, Callum continued to make slow, steady progress, getting stronger and bigger. He was tiny, he took time to grow and develop, but he was a fighter and stronger than he looked – he always got there in the end. As a dad, watching him progress has been a beautiful, sometimes hard, lesson in patience. Looking at him now, you'd have no idea. He's the tallest in his class, physically strong, and shows no signs of the challenges he faced as a baby.

Having come through a neonatal journey and experienced what it was like as a father, and having witnessed the impact it has on the mother, I am so incredibly proud of both Callum and Sarra. There is so much to a premature birth, it probably deserves a book in its own right and I have only touched upon the surface of it. Reflecting back on it now, I realise just how difficult it can be for families for many, many different reasons. It has left me deeply grateful for the medical and nursing staff who saved Sarra and Callum and who guided us through. It was a very difficult experience for Sarra. We were both so focused on Callum that I don't think either of us realised what a huge impact it had on her. She was traumatised by it, both at the time and for many years afterwards. There are days still when it catches my breath to consider what a huge mountain we managed to climb together. Having gone through this with Sarra I think it brought us closer together than ever before.

For a long time, there was never a thought about having a second baby. We felt so lucky that we had all survived the first time around, literally and metaphorically. But they say time is a great healer and in due course, as Callum's health started to improve, we did begin to think about having a brother or sister for him. We considered the possibility of another premature birth, but we felt stronger and equipped with more information that made us better placed to deal with it if it were to happen again.

The second time around, Sarra's pregnancy was very carefully monitored by a consultant, but it still felt like a nervous pregnancy. The weeks ticked by and as we got to twenty-nine, it felt like a truly pivotal moment – we had never made it this far before! Then we reached thirty-two weeks, then thirty-four, by which stage it felt like we could handle anything. It was becoming clear, though, that the dreaded pre-eclampsia was threatening to show again, so a C-section was arranged at thirty-six weeks. The delivery was much smoother, and this time a tiny little girl called Chloe popped out, weighing a diminutive four pounds four ounces. 'She's so huge!' we both exclaimed as she was placed on Sarra's chest. The staff must have thought we were nuts. While there had been some difficult, worrying moments during this pregnancy, it felt a lot less stressful. I'd say we almost enjoyed it.

Within a few days, we were all back home together, with Callum, and it felt like the final piece of the jigsaw had been fitted into place. We felt so lucky to have managed to create a family and our hearts and arms were full.

I used to think other parents were delusional when they said their babies had a particular personality. How can that be? But it's so true, and from a young age I saw Callum and Chloe's different characters shining through. Chloe has that 'second child' confidence, piling in there and getting stuck in, whatever the situation. While she might be quiet at school, don't be fooled. She's loud, noisy and never stops talking at home. She's very funny and a brilliant mimic – a real rascal actually. She's already very determined to master new skills and with that comes a sense of competitiveness. You can see she wants to succeed in whatever she tries and how quickly she gets disheartened if we're doing something like a race in the garden and Callum, Sarra or I get ahead of her. I can see my competitive mentality is like that too. She's so independent and very articulate, especially when expressing her frustrations. She can argue like she is captain of the debating society already, perhaps inherited from her mum's legal brain. She has a keen sense of justice too, particularly when it comes to whether she and her brother have had equal iPad time!

Like his sister, Callum is hilarious, with a wicked sense of humour. He is keenly observant with an eye for detail. He can be more cautious and mindful of hazards, and likes to analyse stuff before getting involved, but when he does settle on something, he goes all in. He is a real thinker and I love how engrossed he can get in specific things, a character trait he shares with me. Recently on holiday, it was anything to do with watersports, out on a paddleboard or kayak, or sailing on a two-man catamaran with an instructor all day long. He loves to find out how things work and shares a passion for aircraft with Sarra's dad, who was in the RAF, with the two of them endlessly practising the radio calls for take-offs and landings for various aircraft.

If Callum and Chloe ever come to read this when they are older, I want them to know how unbelievably proud I am of them and always will be. They are capable of so much, much more than they realise at this young age. I see how kind and loving they are, and I know they will achieve great things. I don't care what that might be, whether they are sporty, arty, musical, academic or not. I simply admire them for who they are – their personalities shine through every day and I know they are caring, loving and emotionally connected to all around them. I love how they already have a strong sense of self and I hope they keep that as they grow older, because with the values they show to me every day, I know they can't go wrong.

Watching them grow and develop is the most wonderful thing. We all constantly tell each other that we love each other. In return, both Callum and Chloe are incredibly affectionate and coming home to be greeted with one of their hugs is among the best aspects of being a parent, even more so when they shout 'Daddy!' and race to me when I've been away for a few days. It's a word I never imagined could have such an impact from two such wee voices.

CHAPTER FIVE

2023

I'M sitting on the flight back from New York and I know what's coming when I land. There is a sense of dread and foreboding, a feeling in the pit of my stomach, long echoed from childhood, of facing fears. But here in this adult world, this is real fear, like a hand around my throat. I'm just days away from chemotherapy and the very word sends a surge of adrenaline through me, a word with a fearsome reputation, and for good reason.

I've heard what it can do to people, how it can ravage the body and leave nothing but a shell of the person that stood before. I've even heard it said that chemo can be worse than the cancer itself. It's perhaps all the more terrifying because I really only know about it through television and films – dealing with it in reality is treading into the unknown. I have no benchmark or past experience to compare it to. How can I?

I'm not ashamed to admit that I'm scared, apprehension building of what's to come and how my body will react. No two people respond the same and I'm told it can change from one round to the next. I know I need a plan, so I decide to view chemotherapy like a gruelling eighteen-week training block, three weeks at a time. But instead of brutal days in the gym and velodrome, this time the challenge will be coping with the consequences of this treatment, the likes of which I have heard so many scary stories about.

In a warped way, there's a small part of me that feels a frisson of excitement too. After weeks of tests, consultations, thinking, talking, planning, pill popping and facing this stark reality, I'm finally doing the first thing that feels properly proactive to repel this deadly disease.

Because of the stage I'm at with the cancer, I've been prescribed one of the most toxic chemotherapy treatments available, the only viable approach to hit the disease where it hurts to stop it growing further. It's odd but bar some aches and pains in my joints, I don't feel all that ill or remotely weakened by the cancer just yet, so I keep reminding myself that I'm physically strong and fit and hope that this might count in my favour.

The days have ticked towards this point – sometimes slowly, sometimes like an uncontrollable runaway train – but then there is a suddenness, a dark jolt when the day finally arrives. Driving to the hospital, it feels like a big black cloud on the horizon, a horrible foreboding as I take the tentative steps from the car to the hospital doors, every footstep feeling heavy and laden with meaning. While the kids know about the cancer now, we're trying to keep it out of the public eye for as long as possible. The good thing about arriving at a hospital is you can put on a face mask as you're heading in – many people are still wearing masks

– so no one recognises me. Going incognito is helped by the fact that the hospital staff have thoughtfully organised a private room for my treatment because they understand how important privacy is at this early stage. I am very grateful for that.

Driving to the hospital for each round can feel like a drag, the journey synonymous with the pain and discomfort that are to follow. It pulls me back to when Callum was tiny, every day a round trip with nothing else in it. But Steve Peters tells me I have to approach it with the mindset that I'm going to blitz cancer and to take that on board, almost try to skip my way there, ready to meet it head on. I slowly begin to get into that frame of mind, to grasp the idea that each time I am fighting back, and that helps as I go through the door. But it's hard, it really does test your mental resolve.

The walk along the corridors is a potential and painful glance into the future. As Sarra and I go from one corridor to the next, all we see are sick people, far sicker than me. There are women with headscarves on, men with haunted eyes; all in all, some really poorly looking souls, and that doesn't help my morale as I'm heading in. There are people a lot further down the line and that's pretty difficult to witness. The natural reaction is to think, *Am I going to be like that one day? Is this what's waiting for me?* It's hard to swallow the lump of fear that gathers in my throat.

Gingerly pushing open the door to the treatment room, I don't know what I'm expecting but the sight hits me hard. This room has far less paraphernalia in it than I was subconsciously expecting. There are no airs and graces, no pictures or vases of fake flowers to soften it. As I cautiously step inside, there in the middle of the room sits a giant, intimidating-looking reclining chair similar to the sort you see at the dentist's, a machine behind it with a screen and the drugs hanging to the side, already prepped and ready to be pumped into me.

But as much as the terror grips me, oddly it feels like a good thing, like pre-race nerves before a major event. I tell myself this is finally the chance to punch back. At last, I can do something proactive to meet this uninvited inhabitant head on; it's the first step towards kicking the can down the road to give me as much time as possible. I feel devastated to be here, but make a feeble attempt not to show it as I am welcomed to the ward and given a tour of the room (well, the chair really) by a warm and friendly nurse. Before long, I am in the chair waiting for the first intake of drugs and to find out how my body will react.

How has it come to this? I think to myself. Then, *I'm about to sit here and get poison pumped into my veins. Fucking hell. How have I ended up in this position?* And it's all happened so fast, or it feels like it. Eight weeks on from that first scan and the dreadful diagnosis and I'm here in this chair. While in a strange way I'm keen to get cracking, I realise that in many ways I haven't come to terms with it all.

Even at his tender age, Callum is acutely aware of what cancer and chemo entail. A friend of ours had a similar treatment and Callum was shocked when he saw her for the first time with no hair. He asked about it a lot at the time and we explained to him about cancer, chemo and hair loss. Little did we ever imagine it would be my turn within months of that conversation. His biggest question, which he keeps asking in a variety of ways, is whether I will lose my hair. My first reaction is light-hearted – 'I've not got much hair as it is, son!' – and I suggest he can help me shave it all off, but he is having none of that. I reassure him that it will grow back but I realise increasingly how big a deal it is for him. I think for him it is THE symbol of cancer and illness. So, I want to keep my hair as much as possible, for my boy.

Not everyone loses their hair through chemo. Plus, treatment allows patients to choose to use a 'cold cap'. Effectively, this is agreeing to have my head frozen shortly before, during and after the treatment, which aids my chances of keeping my hair. I'm already having my hands and feet frozen, to ensure the loss of sensation you experience in your fingers and toes during the chemo doesn't become permanent. They put on big black spongy neoprene mittens and slippers that are frozen to minus twenty-seven degrees Celsius. They come out of the freezer covered in frost and smelling of damp washing. They can provide something similar for my head. By freezing the nerves before the chemo comes into the bloodstream, these contraptions temporarily kill the nerves so there's nothing for the chemicals to damage. So, before the chemo even starts, before any drugs are given, the first step is the cold cap and then the freezing of my fingers and feet.

The nurse presents me with the sci-fi-esque plastic skull cap embossed with furrows arranged in a swirling pattern that looks to me like a brain, into which a machine pumps ice-cold gel. It's almost like a swim cap in shape but with those hard channels it's even more difficult to pull onto your head. This is covered with another cap with a chin strap attached, which pulls it down onto your head to ensure pressure is constant throughout. It's painful before the machine is even switched on, like someone is squeezing your head in a vice.

To make sure the cap is firmly in place, the nurse gives the straps an extra tug, and if it wasn't so serious, I'd be laughing at how ridiculous I look. She turns it on and, oh my God, there isn't a moment to brace myself, the pain is immediate. The Arctic bitterness of cold is upon every inch of my scalp and the pressure is hideous. The inner cap fills immediately and the icy liquid is repeatedly pumped through it so it never warms up. It is almost unbearable, and the first ten minutes are probably the worst because of the shock of it all.

The process begins half an hour before the infusion, then the cap stays on throughout the hour-long infusion and for another twenty minutes afterwards. My initial thought is, *Holy shit, I can't do this for ten minutes, let alone an hour and fifty minutes*. It all feels dehumanising, being trussed up and strapped down, and now the room has become the torture chamber I was scared of. It is hard to get out of this trap, my mind can't fight it. It has stripped me of my dignity and I feel incredibly vulnerable sitting here, unable to move. I can't even wipe away my tears when they fall, and Sarra stands up with a tissue to catch them. And suddenly I'm really emotional again, hit with that repeating wave of *how have I got here, why's it come to this?* I'm sitting there, feeling sorry for myself, like my life is falling apart.

Throughout all this, the nurse hasn't yet stopped talking. She is running through the list of side effects and warning signs to watch out for. The list is endless, and she is just constantly talking, and it isn't helping to soothe how I'm feeling right now.

I'm trying to take sharp inhalations and exhalations of breath but suddenly the bones in my fingertips and toes are so cold it feels like they're going to split open, while the pressure and temperature of the cold cap are torturous. I try to take the lessons learned from a life spent pushing the physical limits while controlling the negative thoughts. I remind myself I could always do one more lap, one more set, one more rep, even one more turn of the pedals, therefore I can do this now. I find myself able to look up at the clock and take it minute by minute, breaking it down to a single lap of the clock face, one at a time. I do one minute, then another, then another, all the while feeling sorry for myself but also thinking of two main motivating factors, using these to stem the tide of self-pity. The first is Callum, who is worried about his daddy's hair falling out. I think back to watching him in his incubator as he struggled for each breath, how I would watch his chest and will it to rise and fall. The second is my great-uncle Andy Coogan and what he was able to endure in his life.

Andy was one of the most remarkable people I ever met. Born in Glasgow towards the end of the First World War, he was an impressive runner whose ambitions on the track were curtailed by the outbreak of the Second World War. Initially posted to India with the Royal Artillery, he was taken captive by the Japanese in Singapore in 1941. Andy was a prisoner of war in Singapore and then Taiwan, incarcerated in hellish conditions for three and a half years, but he had an astonishing ability not just to survive but to have zero resentment towards his captors in the aftermath. Throughout his ordeal, he was surrounded by sickness, starvation and, ultimately, death. He worked in a copper mine and then on the railways, and was barely twenty miles from where the atomic bomb was dropped on Nagasaki. For a period of his imprisonment, he was forced to sleep in a shed in the middle of winter with only rugs on him and the warmth of his fellow prisoners to help fend off the minus temperatures outside. Often, by morning, the body next to him was rigid cold, having finally succumbed to the torture, toil and sickness that ripped through the camps, and died.

As a child, I was in awe of him and his stories, which seemed to be countless. He'd had aspirations to run at the 1948 Olympics, which were denied by war. Early in his army days, he was a soldier in barracks in Edinburgh when he snuck out, unbeknown to his superiors, to race the great American middle-distance runner Sydney Wooderson over a mile at Ibrox and only narrowly came second. Unfortunately for him, his picture was plastered over the next day's *Glasgow Herald* and he got in hot water as a result. But he kept that newspaper cutting on him throughout the war and it proved to his benefit a few years later during his internment when it was uncovered by a prison guard, who was himself a keen runner. From then, the guard would only pretend to hit him during beatings, and also gave him lotion to treat his wounds. Amid all those three and a half years, Andy's ability to endure the most awful treatment – from mock executions to being ordered on two separate occasions to dig his own grave – was astonishing. And his willingness to forgive and never bear a grudge was even more astonishing. These few paragraphs barely do justice to a life so well lived, with so many twists and turns. One of them that really sticks with me was at the end of the war, when queuing to board a plane to take him home at long last, Andy spotted the priest from his local church. He gave up his spot in the queue to help the clergyman safely onto a different aircaft, which meant Andy missed the flight he was originally bound for. The aircraft Andy should have boarded crashed, leaving no survivors. Andy showed unbelievable mental strength to endure it all, and to thrive when he was eventually liberated and his normal life could resume. He was still running and winning medals in Masters events on the track well into his seventies.

He carried the Olympic torch in the build-up to the London 2012 Games and two years later passed me the Queen's Baton at the 2014 Commonwealth Games opening ceremony. It was a tremendous moment for me and I would like to think it was quite a memorable one for him too. He died a few days short of his hundredth birthday. His is a remarkable story and, knowing what he went through, I'm thinking, *What the hell have I got to be sorry about? If Uncle Andy can get through that, I can get through an hour and a half, two hours of a bit of discomfort.* When I try to reframe it in this way, the pain is bearable, like a low level of torture you can endure. And it is going to make this cancer shrink. It is part of the fight. As each minute passes, I get closer to the end, the thinking then being I can't take the cap off as I've got this far already. The alternative is failure.

Thirty minutes in, reclining in my chemo chair in my stylish Mr Freeze cap, gloves and socks, Sarra sitting opposite me, we are ready to start the actual drugs as a cannula pierces my skin and is attached to the machine behind me. They set its rate of secretion and the slow, steady beeps begin as the chemotherapy finally gets under way. It's initially cold as it goes through, but otherwise I don't really feel it. I understand that this infusion of toxic drugs is what is going to effectively poison my body (and the cancer, of course), but at this point I'm just 100 per cent distracted by the strap, so tight on my chin I can't even really speak.

I'm conscious, too, that I have to eat mid-chemo in order to take the next round of tablets, but how do you eat with a chin strap on and both hands immersed in ice-cold gloves? Sarra opens a tuna wrap and tries to feed me, the strap on my chin making it hard to even open my mouth, let alone chew. Eating's the last thing I want to do, but a necessity, and it's astonishing how helpless I feel, unable to carry out this simplest and most natural of tasks for myself.

I pride myself on being polite to people but this is pushing me too far, I can feel I am losing myself. My chimp is well and truly out of the cage and I am on the verge of fight or flight at any given moment. I know I'm shorter and snappier with the nurses than my true self wants to be, especially when all they're trying to do is make me feel comfortable. But even small talk just becomes impossible, and so often it turns to whether I have children, which somehow makes the situation all the harder. *Please, please, please don't talk to me about my children*, I think. I prefer silence; then I am able to go into myself, breathe and just get through this. I can concentrate on what I know about pain – I have the ability to withstand it. I just need to hunker down and focus in on it, moment by moment. Having Sarra there is like a lifeline, I couldn't imagine doing this alone; I know she might feel helpless, but she continually tends to my hands and feet while in the mittens, while my eyes are shut tight as I focus on coping with the pain. Despite my eyes being closed, I'm aware Sarra has her gaze locked onto my face for any wince or flicker that might suggest I need something. She is constantly trying to read my signals and respond to them. When someone enters the room, she handles it and politely asks to speak outside – anything that will help me remain focused on enduring the pain.

Occasionally (and with my mute nod of approval) she slips

a mint humbug into my mouth to suck on. She is ready with warm socks to push onto my frozen feet as soon as the chemo ends. The nurses too are vital, and despite my chimp's inclination to snap, I am so grateful for their presence; I need them to know how much I appreciate them as they check on me and the equipment. With them at hand, I can trust everything is OK.

The pain in my fingertips is like someone's driving a stake between my fingers and fingernails. The discomfort is constant and unrelenting and I'm still counting it down, minute by excruciating minute. And then, after almost two hours, it is over. The machines are turned off and I'm detached from all the tubes and frozen garments. The relief is sudden and immediate. I know people endure way worse and I don't want to moan – I'm grateful I'm getting this treatment. My competitive instinct makes me feel proud at having completed round one and I'm already thinking about how to improve my performance for round two. This feels strangely comforting: I have an approach I know I will be able to use. Mentally and physically exhausted, I'm sent home with boxes of pills and instructions for what to do, just in case of a severe reaction, and in case I feel sick.

I come home and get straight back on the gym bike. I want to keep my routine as normal as I can, to remain active despite all this. I have been telling myself I won't be bedridden, that my intention is to be up and about in the ensuing days, to give me a further sense I'm fighting this. But it feels like that's in the past, the chemo is in me now and I'm just bracing myself for what comes next. I feel OK to get on the bike but I feel I'm on a ticking time bomb and I don't know what is in store for me in the days ahead.

I have a very broken sleep that night and when the first symptoms come, it's the pain in my stomach that hits hardest, leading to horrible, constant diarrhoea. It's difficult to know at this stage if that's the chemo or the bone-strengthening injection they gave me beforehand.

I quickly develop a horrendous temperature, shivering and sweating, and there are endless trips back and forth to the toilet. At some point, I'm left wondering, *How much more is there? There can't be any still to come.* But I'm still clinging to the positives: at least I'm not vomiting. I hate being sick, I've always hated it from when I was a young boy. I'm feeling bad at this point, but more alarming is the prospect of it getting a lot worse. If someone could predict the future and map out the trajectory of how bad I am going to feel, I think that would help. Not knowing how long I'll be stuck in this state and how much worse it'll get is a mental battle. As a rule of thumb, they say it's normally a week of feeling bad, a week of starting to come out of it and then a third week where you feel relatively normal again. By the last few days, you're meant to be feeling OK . . . and then you start all over again with round two. I try to remember this.

The list of potential side effects we're told about is so long, it's hard to keep track. There may be mouth ulcers, rashes, dry eyes and mouth, fever, my fingernails might fall off, and if they go black I must phone and let them know. If there's a tingling in my toes, again pick up the phone, although that might be the tumour in my back. I'm on tenterhooks for every change in my body and, all the while, there's also the very real threat of sepsis. Being sick is normal, I'm told, but the combination of sickness with diarrhoea and temperature is enough to call the doctor immediately. It might be sepsis, it might not. The warnings are a reminder that this is a dangerous medicine.

Following that first round of chemo, I'm lucky, and after maybe five days I start to turn the corner. But I don't want to jinx things as I know the effects are cumulative and for round two I might not be so lucky. When I'm in the depths of it, it's most like a really bad flu, the first few days just aching, a struggle to do anything, every part of my body hurts, I have a high temperature, I can't eat anything, only really sip water. It's horrible, but eventually I get through it, and one morning I get up and realise, *Oh, I slept OK last night*, and that I feel better than I did yesterday. And then I'm out the other side of the chemo effects, thinking it was bad, but it could have been worse. I'm constantly reminding myself it could have been worse.

The doctors tell me gentle exercise can be beneficial for recovery. So, as I did that first day, every day I force myself onto the indoor bike in my garage gym. It might seem stupid, but I want to try to do something, to be proactive rather than just passive, even if in the first couple of days it's just fifteen minutes slowly turning my legs. Each time, it makes

My first Olympic gold, Athens, 2004.

Sarra, my sister, Mum and Dad at the Olympic keirin final in Beijing, 2008.

The keirin, London 2012, and that roar when you win . . .

On the red carpet with Sarra in the dizzying aftermath.

At my retirement press conference with Sarra, 2013.

My uncle Andy surprising me by standing up to pass the torch on the opening night of the Glasgow Commonwealth Games, 2014.

Busted with my phone, live on air! Clare Balding being a total pro, as usual.

Bringing Callum home after eight weeks in hospital.

Callum and me holding Chloe.

Trying to style it out after crashing the Nissan at the Goodwood Festival of Speed: three and a half haystacks deep!

The culmination of another childhood dream: racing at Le Mans.

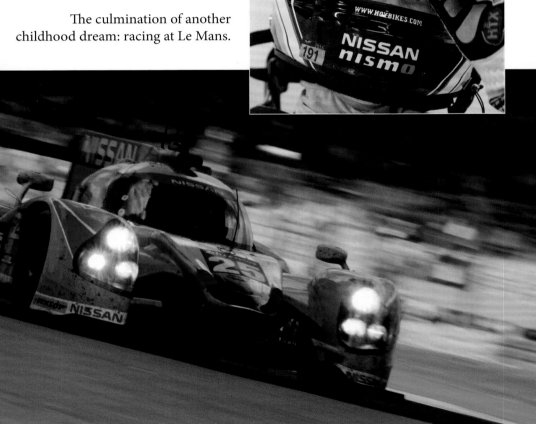

The morning after the diagnosis. Pasting on a smile for the kids.

New York, November 2023: a bucket list trip, but a very difficult one.

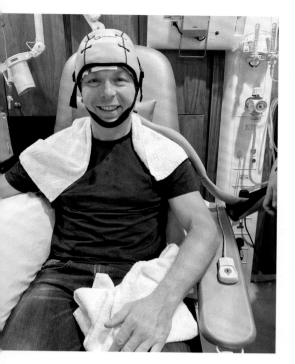

The cold cap. My nemesis.

Getting back on the bike after a chemo
session, a key part of my recovery.

The tree the kids drew me, filled with
blossoms to mark the end of chemo.

Reaching the top of Mount Nakkerd on our family holiday in Thailand, a personal milestone for me.

Opening the velodrome at the Paris Olympics in 2024. It was a joy to be there.

me feel better – maybe mentally more than physically – to get a slight sweat on and feel mildly active. I desperately don't want to let go of the feeling of being fit and active.

Each of the six rounds of chemo is different: both the treatment schedule and the after-effects. The second time around, while sitting in the chair ready to go with the frozen membrane on my skull, I naively think, *I've done it once, I can do it again and it'll be easier at the second time of asking because I know what to expect.* But almost as soon as the infusion begins, there's something wrong. My body has an allergic reaction to the chemo drugs, it feels like a sudden pressure on my chest, I'm unable to breathe. I'm given anti-histamines and cortisol to treat it. The whole time the ice cap is on, with its vice-like grip, and I'm told we'll go again with attempt two at the chemo drugs an hour later. The infusion has to be slowed because of my adverse reaction, meaning I end up wearing the cap for nigh on four hours.

Even with Callum and Uncle Andy in my head, I come close to quitting and removing the ice cap – it would be so much more bearable without it – but I finally make it through. Sarra, as always, is a huge part of my strength throughout the treatments. I simply can't imagine doing this without her unwavering love and support. Again, I try to remind myself that, despite all of this, I'm still so lucky.

As the equipment is removed after round two, the relief isn't immediate. I am broken, absolutely shattered, no cele-bration, no feeling of *well done.* I just feel so drained and so low, one of the toughest days mentally I've experienced in my lifetime, and the thought that it could be this bad or worse in the next round is terrifying. I tell Sarra I think I won't do the ice cap again. She tells me not to make any decision about it now when I'm feeling so ragged by it. 'It's over for today,' she says. 'Wait and make the decision next time,' she tells me. She doesn't care about my hair but she also knows the value of having it – for Callum, and for privacy amongst other reasons. I drag myself up from the chair, Sarra hugs me and tells me she's proud of me and we head home. The waiting game begins for the aftermath.

The fallout this time feels like I've been stabbed in the guts, the sharpest pain I can think of, like something's going to spit out of me like an alien. I'm unable to sleep all night, hunched over the floor on all fours, and Sarra tries, offering to help, but there's nothing she can do, nothing that gives me any relief.

The other thing is, I just can't do anything, but I can't do nothing. I'm too restless to sit watching the TV and can't concentrate on reading or looking at my phone so I prowl around the house like a caged animal, engulfed in this incredible fatigue – but when I succumb to it and take to my bed, I can't sleep either. Sometimes, I go to bed at the same time as the kids and then I'm bolt upright at 10.30pm, wide awake, with the whole night ahead of me. It's like the old days when the kids were babies keeping us up all night, only this time I'm the culprit.

There are all sorts of other peculiar effects throughout the process, one of which is the sensation of a jolt of electricity going down my leg. I remember a similar but much milder sensation at the height of my cycling career when I'd done particularly hard sessions; it's like I'm building towards a sudden jump in my legs, the sort that mainly happens when I'm lying in bed at night, like two or three seconds of being charged up. It's as if I'm in A&E, they shout 'charge', and my legs kick the duvet up in the air. Apparently, it's to do with the central nervous system being overloaded during chemo – just one of the many exhausting and unnerving side effects on the long list.

And all the while, I have this unquenchable thirst. A dry mouth doesn't sound so bad, does it? But I drink a whole glass of water and I'm immediately parched, nothing helps and my mouth remains like sandpaper with no moisture, my tongue constantly sticking to the roof of it. Then there are the fluctuations in temperature: I'm freezing cold, wrap myself up, and the next minute I kick the covers off in a hot flush. There are mouth ulcers, dry skin, cracked fingers, being unable to blink for the lack of moisture. By themselves, they're all manageable; combined, it's relentless and exhausting. But I remind myself it's good, it's a symptom of the drugs doing their thing. It's like this wild rodeo ride or fighting a war of attrition and I'm simply thinking, if I can just keep a grip, hold on a little bit longer, it'll eventually come to an end.

Even the simple pleasures are erased. I love my coffee – in reality, I'm not ashamed to admit I'm a bit of a coffee bore – but I sip my usual favourite and it tastes horrendous, like the milk's off. Despite the changes in taste, for the most part I don't lose my appetite and generally eat well when I can.

Each day, I am managing to get on my bike and I try to push on through, as if I'm a cyclist back in training. It's not to say I'm not feeling pain but that doesn't matter, I tell myself: I need to keep moving. Some days are tougher than others during the three-week period between each chemo treatment but, as those three weeks progress, I push myself with greater challenges physically and mentally. I ride on the bike on Zwift* every day, even leading virtual Doddie Aid motor neurone disease (MND) charity Zwift Rides every Sunday throughout January. I feel proud at being able to keep these going and think about the big man Doddie Weir himself as I pedal away, giving me the determination to keep going despite feeling so weak. By the end of chemo I will realise that I have only missed five days on the bike since the day I was diagnosed.

I am also pleased that I am able to do some work throughout this period too. I continue to work on my podcast, *Sporting Misadventures*, with my friend Matt, I do occasional appearances for sponsors, film adverts, I present my keynote speech at events in person or over Zoom, all things that make life seem more normal.

Sarra and I go for walks and I do track days in the car. I

---

* Zwift is indoor cycling, connecting users via an online virtual platform.

try to find things to occupy my mind, to take me away from thinking about cancer, even if only for short periods at a time. The most effective thing is driving on track, such is the total concentration that that requires. I can go for twenty to thirty minutes at a time immersed in that world and find it a huge relief and break from the mental load. I also spend time connecting with close friends who know of my situation, in particular David Smith.

David is a good friend and a Paralympic champion. I've watched in awe of him, his ability to just keep on coming back from adversity, battling against repeated cancerous tumours as well as dealing with a spinal cord injury and the multiple surgeries that entailed. We text each other a lot during that time and he provides me with unconditional support. He understands so much of what I'm going through and he faces a daily battle with his mind to overcome the pain and disability he faces every day. Our friendship deepens even though he is on the other side of the world for much of this period. I'm complaining about feeling tired and a bit rubbish and while I can't do everything I could before, unlike David I still have full mobility, I'm still riding my bike and able to spend time with my kids. It is David who helps me remember there are so many things to feel lucky about. Even at this low ebb, there are still moments of utter joy.

I'm not delusional enough to think that just because I could ride my bike around fast in anticlockwise circles, I can somehow beat this inevitable disease. And I'm also not naive enough to think that what I'm going through is somehow unique. That's a thought pattern that helps keep morale up at a time when I feel alone in my struggle, knowing that so many other people are coming in and out of hospital every day and yet they're still pushing on. And I'm trying to be more mindful of other people, and realise just how many stories there are to be inspired by.

CHAPTER SIX

2013–24

Iᴛ's Boxing Day 1981. Curtains drawn, overhead light switch flicked off, I gently place two Porsche 911s – one silver, one gold, complete with little headlights – down on the track, then tentatively press the controllers in my hands and watch, mesmerised, as they loop around my brand new Scalextric Le Mans 24hr edition track, lap after lap. I have always loved the 911 from that moment as a five-year-old – in miniature and in real life.

Unlike the other Scalextric cars that I had, these Porsches had working lights on the front, and I had to ask my dad why this was. He explained that they were inspired by the actual cars which took part in the 'World's Greatest Endurance Race', the ultimate test of man and machine – the 24 Hours of Le Mans. My eyes widened as he told me how teams of three drivers would race flat out through day and night, only pausing to change tyres, refuel and swap drivers every few hours. And so, my obsession began. 'When do they go to sleep?' I asked, still bemused by the concept, and to help me understand, we sat down and watched it for real. I was mesmerised and it lodged in my head, this little nugget of motorsport magic. Whenever it came around each year, I would watch it on TV, fascinated by the seeming impossibility of it. There was never a sense that I might do it one day, it was more like watching *Top of the Pops*: an amazing spectacle to enjoy. I was about as likely to become a pop star and make a chart-topping record as I was to be a racing driver.

I wasn't an avid watcher of motorsport as a kid, but there was just so much of it on terrestrial TV in those days when you flicked it on, whether that was Le Mans, F1, the World Rally Championship or even rallycross from Lydden Hill. I didn't go to watch anything live and it never felt like something I'd get into. I was aware early on it was prohibitively expensive.

And it wasn't like we were petrolheads as a family. My dad's car choice was always centred around how frugal it was, basically a mode of transport to get him and me to BMX races. There wasn't a lot of spare money kicking around so it was a question of which car was the cheapest to buy and run. Usually, the answer was a Citroën BX diesel; we must have had three or four of them over the years. I had a real soft spot for this car; it wasn't fast or powerful or even mildly cool back then, but it took my dad and me all over the UK and even to Europe for races and we had so many adventures and fun times on those trips. I do also remember it occasionally conking out and moments spent stranded on the side of the road beside a broken-down car. One time, driving back from a race in Southampton, I'd fallen asleep and it must have been the middle of the night when I woke up, aware of a change in the noise of the car's engine. The clutch had gone and Dad was jamming his way through the gears to keep it rolling to get us home. We always made it home . . . eventually!

I was a teenager by the time Colin McRae, a fellow Scot, took the rally scene by storm, and in 1995 he became the first British driver to win the World Rally Championship. Colin quickly became one of my sporting heroes and was responsible for a new-found obsession with motorsport and cars.

In my early thirties I started doing track days for fun at my local circuit, Oulton Park. I would do them in the cycling off-season; just a handful of days a year, a hobby that gave me a huge amount of pleasure, but one that I never thought would lead to anything.

Years later, in late 2012, I was honoured to be asked to film a BBC documentary about Colin McRae's career and, while shooting a scene at Oulton Park, I met Roger Green, who would go on to become a good friend of mine. I recognised him as a journalist from *Evo* magazine but he was now working for a British sportscar company called Radical. He asked if I had ever thought about racing. I hadn't, I had absolutely no idea how to get into it beyond enjoying the odd track day. The concept of doing anything like that seemed impossible at that time.

Roger told me that Radical was running a novice-only championship the following year and asked if I'd like to get involved. He said they could provide a car, tuition and get me qualified with a race licence. I didn't need to be asked twice and jumped at the chance.

Within a couple of weeks I was at Bedford Autodrome in a Radical SR1 with Andy Wallace, the Le Mans 1988 winner, in the passenger seat as my driver coach! I'd say there are some racing drivers who lack patience as instructors, but Andy was the total opposite. We'd get in the car, him in the driving seat for two or three laps illustrating the point he was trying to get across or the specific skill he wanted to teach me. Then he'd hop out and we'd change over. We chose Bedford for my first lesson because it's essentially an airfield: flat, wide open and with almost nothing to hit. I very nearly became the exception to the rule, though, when I lost the car on braking, touched the white line, which was slightly damp, did a 360 spin narrowly missing the only solid thing around, a tyre wall on the back straight, by a few feet.

When the car finally came to a halt, we sat there momentarily in silence. Andy quietly and calmly said, 'Well, that was exciting!' and focused on the one positive he could find: 'You managed to get your foot on the clutch before the engine stalled, well done.' He got me to put the car back into first gear and off we went again, as though nothing had happened. It was such a remarkable response when my own adrenaline levels were sky high. Andy's advice was to pick one element to work on during a particular lap, such as a corner where I'd made a mistake and simply needed to brake later. Otherwise, there was just too much to think about. The key was to focus on the section I was struggling with the most until I got it right and then shift my attention to the next problem. It was the sort of game plan I really enjoyed and I realised I had truly caught the racing bug.

Proper racing drivers doing a lap on the track or in the simulator make it look so simple. It's like a professional musician playing an instrument and making it look effortless, then a passionate amateur picking it up and making sounds like a tortured cat. Similarly with the racing driving – particularly early on, I would often be mystified . . . how do they do that? It made me more determined than ever to learn quickly and I saw big improvements almost from the outset. This was refreshing, to be back on the steep part of the learning curve for a new skill. It had been such a long time since I'd made major improvements in cycling; once I was at World level there wasn't huge headroom and the steps up were always tiny fractions. Here I was taking chunks off my lap times every time I got into the car.

My first goal when it came to motorsport was not to be useless and, after that, to try to be competitive. Essentially, it didn't matter – this wasn't going to be a career, I was never going to become a Formula One driver. I was just doing it for the challenge to see how good I could get and because I loved the excitement, the speed, the adrenaline, the nerves before a race, the competition and having a go at chipping away at lap times.

I liked the contrast to the cycling. On the bike, you need to have the right bike and equipment, but it's 99 per cent down to you on the day. In motorsport, the percentage of what's down to the driver is much lower. For example, put the best driver in the world, Max Verstappen, in an Alpine and he's not about to win a Grand Prix. So I had to learn pretty quickly that it wasn't just about me, motorsport is very much about the team. As the driver, I had a role to play within it and I therefore wanted to be the best I could to contribute to the overall effort.

In April 2013 I went to Brands Hatch for practice a week before my first ever race in the SR1 Cup. It was one of those wonderful spring days where the sun was finally out, the temperature around 19 or 20 degrees – perfect, after having not felt warmth on us outside in months. Even now, that day sticks in my mind. I was trying to get sub-fifty seconds for a lap; I had got close, but couldn't quite duck under that mark. With my final lap before the chequered flag, I finally strung together a committed lap without mistakes and dipped under that time. I was genuinely elated and came in as though I'd just won a Grand Prix. This wasn't about anyone else but solely about achieving my personal goal. That year I went on to finish fourth overall in the championship, with a podium finish in my last race. I was utterly hooked on this new sport and so happy that I'd discovered another passion.

At that stage, I still thought it would only be a hobby, a fun thing to do, and that with Andy's help I might just get a little bit quicker, which would be satisfying for me, but nothing more. I never saw it as a replacement for cycling, it just happened to fill that gap in my life which craved speed and adrenaline and kept the competitive juices flowing.

At the end of 2013, Nissan came on board as a sponsor for the Rio Olympics in 2016 and signed me as an ambassador for this campaign. Through this connection, I met Darren Cox, founder of the GT Academy, which gave players of the Sony PlayStation game *Gran Turismo* a chance for a genuine racing career on track. Darren had heard that I'd caught the motor racing bug and suggested I come for a test day at Silverstone so they could have a look at me on track and see if there might be some racing opportunities in the future. This was essentially an audition and so I was incredibly excited and rather nervous about this chance to get my foot in the door with a manufacturer team.

Jann Mardenborough was the poster boy of GT Academy; he'd won his way through from 90,000 entrants to take the top prize and become a real-life professional racing driver for Nissan. He had already finished on the podium at Le Mans earlier that year and in doing so established himself as a serious talent in the sportscar world. He and I were tasked with setting a lap time of the national circuit at Silverstone in a 350Z GT4. It's a short lap, maybe fifty-two seconds in a car like that, and Jann set the benchmark on his first run. I went out and was fractionally quicker, and I could see they were clearly thinking *that can't be right!*

So Jann went out for a second run and sure enough he beat my time. But, it was close enough that they said, 'We've got something we can work with here.' It wasn't a *wow, this kid's got talent* moment, but nor had I made an idiot of myself on the track. And then they delivered the line: 'We think we can get you on the startline at Le Mans in three years' time.' The Scalextric kid inside of me was gobsmacked. I jumped at it and was thrilled with the idea but didn't imagine it could actually happen. So I humoured them, thinking to myself there was never a chance I would make it there, but at least I'd have fun seeing how far I could go and getting the chance to drive some pretty awesome machinery along the way.

And so began this next three-year journey. The step from the little Radical SR1 car I'd been racing with, weighing just 500 kilograms and powered by a Hayabusa motorbike engine, to the wheel of a GT3 Nissan GT-R, weighing two and a half times more, was monumental. It had a V6 550 horse-power turbo-charged engine, slick tyres, ABS (anti-lock braking system), traction control and all sorts of different driver aids. It was huge, an absolute beast, a monster of a machine in comparison to the delicacy of the lightweight car I'd been racing previously. In 2014 I raced it in the British GT Championship, a race series for the best GT cars and drivers in the country. I was in the GT3 Pro/Am category alongside my teammate Alex Buncombe. Each race would see a pitstop halfway through with a driver change and refuel just like Le Mans. Every race was a learning experience and I felt like I progressed massively throughout the season.

It wasn't without drama though, notably at the Goodwood

Festival of Speed where the great and good of motorsport gather each year. It's like a Who's Who of motorsport stars and cars past and present. It was around the time that social media was beginning to really take off so everyone had their smartphones out recording it all, plus the whole thing was streamed live over the internet. I'd been lucky enough to be asked to drive Nissan's limited-edition variant of the road-going GT-R, twice the price of the regular car, with carbon fibre alterations to lighten it and more downforce. There were just two of them in the whole country and the one I was driving was owned by the Nissan CEO Andy Palmer, who was yet to drive it. It was brand new. So, there I was making the car's debut, able to showcase it up and down the hill. On the Thursday and Friday I did a few demo runs up the hill with some passengers alongside me and then came Saturday's 'Supercar Shoot-out', a chance for the manufacturers to show-case their latest models to the world and demonstrate how fast they are.

It's almost a minute-long course – sometimes more, sometimes less, depending on how quick your car is – where giant hay bales act as barriers and it's up to you to clock the quickest time possible. I really wanted to show what the car was capable of now that I was beginning to rub shoulders with these pro racing drivers, and I felt like I'd earned the right to be there. My heart was pounding as I waited for my turn on the start line, feeling pretty stressed as I waited for ages in the queue, and suddenly I was there, ready to go. I got a really clean start and, going into the first corner, I could tell I was quicker than normal with a controlled slide as I got on the power. The car balance felt good, I felt like it was going really well and a decent time was within my grasp. I exited those opening corners faster than I expected and then I was soon hurtling down the main straight past Goodwood House.

Next up was a left-hander, which is unsighted, so you have to brake before you can see the apex of the bend. It's changed now, but there were no braking boards back then and you had to use instinct and judgement to pick the perfect moment to brake. I remember pulling into fifth gear and suddenly thinking I'd never made it to fifth at this point in my previous demo runs. Part of me was thinking this was a great sign, another part was going, *oh my God, what did they say about this corner?* It came back to me in a flash – *if you see the corner and you've not braked, it's too late.* As that thought popped into my head over the crest of the hill, with my foot flat to the floor, I spotted the corner and jumped on the brakes, but it was utterly futile. It was too late.

Braking did nothing on the track to slow my progress, even less as I went straight on into the grass, which felt like sheet ice, and suddenly the hay bales were coming at me at an alarmingly fast rate. I thought, *oh my God, I'm going in.* I'd never had a proper crash before and time slowed down, my brain asking what was going to happen. *Am I going to die here?* I thought. I had a helmet on, airbags, and of course I was going to be fine, but I didn't know that as I hurtled forward to the fast-approaching hay bales at 80mph. I hit one row of hay bales, then ploughed through another, then smashed through a third, and finally came to a rest wedged into the fourth.

Just before crashing, I braced myself by taking my hands off the steering wheel. In F1, when all eventualities have been tried and the drivers know they're going into the barriers, they always take their hands off the steering wheel. The force that goes through the wheels and up into the steering wheel is so powerful it'll break your thumbs. So, I pulled my hands away, shut my eyes, took a deep breath and waited for the impact. The bang as I hit the hay bales was like a bomb going off, followed by a second bang, which was the explosion of the airbag, but my eyes were shut so I wasn't really aware of that happening. By the time I'd made it through three and a half hay bales, I'd achieved something of a record. No one had ever crashed that deep before at Goodwood.

This ignominious record stood until last year, when someone broke it and made it into a fourth. For once I was delighted to see a record of mine broken by someone else! When I finally came to a stop, I had this ringing in my ears and, as a cloud of dust from the hay slowly began to settle, there was this feeling of utter horror at what I'd done to this beauty of a car. I initially thought I'd hide in the car until everyone had gone home, wait until it was dark and then sneak off. I didn't want to face the public. I felt so embarrassed and ashamed, convinced everyone would think I was a complete idiot, having been given the privilege of driving such an amazing car – that I was just a reckless buffoon, not taking it seriously enough, just playing at this sport.

But I had to face up to it – I was in full view of the entire crowd. I'm not quite sure why, but, as I got out of the car, I performed a little bow, was checked over by the medical team and then put on my baseball cap and sunglasses for my walk of shame back to the drivers' club. People were making jokes and taking pictures (I lost count of how many times I was called 'Sir Chris HAY') and then I saw Andy Palmer coming towards me . . . My heart sank, and I knew I'd just have to apologise and hope he understood it was a genuine mistake. 'Are you OK?' he asked. Sheepishly, I replied, 'Fine, I'm so sorry.' Rather than be annoyed, he said simply, 'Don't apologise, we all make mistakes. We can replace cars, not people. As long as you're OK, that's all that matters.' What a thoroughly decent bloke. He then pointed out that the car was getting great publicity with its incredible robustness and safety, bearing in mind what I'd just put it through in my high-speed brush with those hay bales: always a positive PR story to be had, no matter the occasion!

We had the traditional big Goodwood ball that night, with all the legends of motorsport: Stirling Moss, Jackie Stewart, Derek Bell – a real Who's Who. But after what had happened, I didn't want to go – I was mortified. After the crash, the racing had to be halted for forty-five minutes while they made repairs, so everyone was well aware of what I'd done. Everyone was talking about me, and not for the right reasons; I felt uncomfortable and embarrassed. I managed to get to the ball, as I was obliged to sit at the Nissan table with their top executives who had just flown in from Japan. Oh god.

One of the journalists I knew came up to me, laughing hysterically and asking, 'What were you doing, what happened?' Others said not to worry, it happens to the best of us, but this made me feel worse because it only reinforced to me that I couldn't be compared to these professionals. When chatting to Dario and Marino Franchitti, Scottish racing legends, Marino kindly tried to save my blushes by wondering out loud whether there was a problem with the ABS. It was nice of him, but this was very much all on me, and I knew it.

I went up the hill the next day in the other GT-R NISMO and took it really steady, my only focus just to keep the car on the black stuff, but my confidence had taken as big a dent as the Nissan. *Is this really for me?* I remember asking myself time and again. *Do I really want to do this?* I knew I had to be committed and brave, but how would I really know where the line was between bravery and stupidity? I needed both skill and judgement and in that moment I wasn't sure if I had either. Also in the back of my mind was the unavoidable thought that I could seriously hurt myself, or someone else for that matter. It was a hard few days where I really questioned it all and could easily have pulled the plug on motorsport there and then.

These dips, I knew, were inevitable, especially in something so new and so different. It was really quite simple: I'd lost my confidence and simply had to get back on the horse. My next race was just two weeks after my high-profile prang and was taking place at Spa-Francorchamps – one of the most intimidating tracks in the world, hidden deep in the beautiful Belgian Ardennes and one I'd never been to before, beyond the simulator. I ended up arriving through the wrong gate, right next to Eau Rouge. Looking at this infamous hill in the pouring rain, I realised that TV didn't do justice to the completely blind crest. If I couldn't get past a few hay bales, how was I going to master something as complex and challenging as this?

We had some issues with the car in practice, so I only managed a couple of laps in the wet, but somehow my teammate for the weekend, Wolfgang Reip, and I qualified in the top four. We ended up finishing second overall in a field of forty cars, an utterly amazing race, and of course all my worries and lack of confidence just totally evaporated. Only the championship leaders Marco Attard and Alex Sims finished ahead of us. I crossed the line utterly elated, properly over the moon, getting to spray champagne on the podium at Spa, going from an awful low two weeks before at Goodwood to this. I'd fully got the bug for racing now.

The following year in 2015 I took the next step towards the Le Mans dream with Ginetta and their Nissan-powered LMP3 car, competing in the European Le Mans Series. This was serious stuff, a Le Mans-style car and another new learning experience to understand downforce and how to adapt my driving style to make the most of this invisible phenomenon. I raced alongside pro driver Charlie Robertson, a young superstar and fellow Scot. He was incredible behind the wheel and I learned so much from him despite him being half my age. We had a remarkable year, winning three rounds and one second place to win the overall LMP3 championship. It was a team effort, with Charlie doing the heavy lifting and we had a weapon of a car, but technically I was a European Champion again!

I felt so fortunate to have a second stab at racing of any sort and to be able to quench that thirst for speed and adrenaline. I focused my all on being the best amateur on the grid at every race I did. I was acutely aware of my level compared to the pros, but I absolutely loved being part of this world.

Despite the success of the 2015 season in the back of my mind, I kept wondering if Le Mans was perhaps a step too far. This was serious stuff, with certain manufacturer teams reputedly having budgets upwards of US$100 million per season to be competitive for the overall victory. I wasn't on one of those high-budget teams, but I would be racing wheel to wheel with some of the best drivers and teams on the planet and this was intimidating to say the least.

Even turning up for the official 'test' prior to raceweek and getting to drive practice laps on the iconic circuit for the first time was overwhelming. This wasn't like turning up at Oulton Park in my Caterham for a public track day, Le Mans' 'Circuit de la Sarthe' is made up of a combination of public roads and a purpose-built track, so you can only drive it once a year and only if you're involved in the twenty-four-hour race. I remember heading out of the pitlane and onto the track the very first time, in torrential rain, feeling completely out of my depth.

I remember at points thinking, *what the hell am I doing here?* It had all the hallmarks of a classic midlife crisis, and I had these swirling thoughts of *grow up and get out before you hurt yourself.* I was a dad now, I had responsibilities to my family. But, ultimately, that fear and heightened state of awareness was like an accentuated survival instinct: it helped mitigate the dangers; I was never reckless, and I certainly didn't have any sort of death wish. What I did enjoy though was the sense of overcoming the fear. It was akin to my cycling career, having a challenge to overcome and working out how to do it. And the adrenaline in the aftermath was almost identical.

You never lose sight of the fact that you are in control of a powerful and potentially dangerous machine, but you try to push this thought out of your consciousness and focus only on how to get it round each lap as quickly as you possibly can. It's still not an instinctive skill for me at this stage; I'm having to remind myself of the basic process to get the best out of myself:

'. . . spot the braking point . . . there it is . . . get ready annnnd . . . BRAKE, down 1, 2, 3 gears . . . spot the apex, release the brake, send the car into the apex, pick up the throttle, spot the exit kerb, release the steering lock . . . and you're through the corner!'

Every split second counts on every single corner. There are thirty-eight corners at Le Mans, and you might complete

350 laps in twenty-four hours. That's 13,300 corners in one race. If you lost a tenth of a second on every corner that would equate to a loss of over twenty-two minutes by the end of the race. When you think of it that way you realise it's actually a twenty-four-hour sprint.

The challenge had been to learn the skills required to drive at that level up against guys who started karting aged five and had twenty years or more of race experience. It was second nature to them. I'd taken it up three years ago and had probably only done twenty-five races in my life by that point. I wanted to treat it like my cycling career where I would train five hours a day, six days a week, but here I only had the opportunity to drive the car every couple of weeks. In other words it was like trying to learn a musical instrument in your thirties but only getting a chance to play it once a month. That was my level of preparation for the biggest motorsport race of my life.

There was a rawness of emotion to my Le Mans experience. No one was making me do this, I had chosen to put myself into this position . . . and I was hooked. This was a beast at my disposal, and it was like some sort of motorsport rodeo. I didn't want to tiptoe around but, similarly, I didn't want to overstep the mark, not respect the car and its power – and find myself heading towards a wall rather than a hay bale this time.

The French are so good at putting on these unique sporting events that almost transcend sport, like the Tour de France or the Dakar Rally. All the locals have a passion for it and it draws people from all around the world to witness the spectacle firsthand. Each year 300,000 spectators are littered around every segment of this massive track. Very few racing drivers ever have the privilege of racing the 24 Hours of Le Mans and yet here I was, some former Olympic cyclist, up against some of the best in the world. It's a bit like getting to play at the World Cup alongside the likes of Lionel Messi or Kylian Mbappé. But instead of Messi and Mbappé, I had these superstars of F1 and sports cars alongside me. Quite a bizarre thought for the five-year-old Scalextric fan inside me.

The LMP2 Ligier I drove at Le Mans is comfortably the best car I've ever experienced. It had a tiny door that meant you had to climb in feet first – it was all a bit 'Dukes of Hazzard' style as you squeezed through this comically small aperture to get in. Once there, it was highly claustrophobic and unlike anything you might experience in a road car. The setup was such that the driver lies flat on the floor, shoulders higher than knees but not by much. It was like setting foot inside the cockpit of an airplane with 101 buttons staring back at me: oil pressure, tyre pressure, delta of times of the laps, rev lights, shift lights letting you know when to change gear. When I first saw it, I was totally overwhelmed and thought I'd never learn how to do it, but in time you grow to love it. When fired up, even with earplugs in, it's so incredibly loud, and the noise doesn't just go through your ears but throughout your whole body with the vibrations. It sounded so angry, like it wanted to kill you, so there was a serious intimidation factor to it all. I had to treat it with respect and be on my toes.

I'd love to say that when the day came for the 24 Hours of Le Mans itself, I approached it without trepidation, but that would be a lie. There was the worry of getting hurt. There was the worry of letting down my teammates, Michael Munemann and Andrea Pizzitola, but also that the car might break down or go off track before I could get behind the steering wheel and all this build-up for the last three years would be for nothing.

The plan for the race was simple: Andrea would start the race, complete roughly two hours (or two tanks of fuel) in the hot seat, then he would jump out and hand over to me. I'd do the same duration of stint and after that I'd jump out for Michael to take his turn. It would then repeat in this order until we had driven for twenty-four hours. Easy. In theory.

When I finally got into the car and pulled out of the pitlane onto the track, I felt like I'd been released into the wild. The wait was over.

Each stint began the same. As soon as the tyres and fuel were done, the mechanic at the front of the car flipped the big lollipop sign from STOP to GO and I leapt out of the pits with the speed limiter set at 60km/h; I crossed the pitlane exit line, deactivated the limiter and then I was *off*. From then onwards, I was just living in the moment, desperately thinking about what was happening ahead but also being proactive. It was just so unimaginably exciting coming into the Porsche Curves from Indianapolis – heading in, a slight brake into fifth gear, and all your expectations were that the car would spin off. But it stuck to the ground, this incredible machine that I had to trust and whose downforce seemed to make the impossible possible. I just had to put my faith in it, and it defied all logic by sticking to the track. And the whole time, there were concrete walls on either side of me and I knew that, if I got anything wrong, it would be expensive, ruinous for my race and that of my co-drivers, and with the potential to cause me a major injury.

With every hyper-present eventuality running through my head, I was clear of all other thoughts, with no ability to think of anything or anyone else – I only had the capacity to consider the track ahead and focus on how I would negotiate it. I don't know if the very elite drivers have time to think of other stuff, but my brain was at full capacity, unable to ponder anything beyond what was in front of me or in the cockpit of this powerful machine. It was such a perfect example of living in the moment: at that point, it felt like nothing else existed in this world. Although, having said that, I do remember during my three-hour night stint from midnight to 3am seeing the leaders coming up to lap me. Mark Webber in the Porsche LMP1 and Toyota's Kamui Kobayashi were battling it out and for a split second I felt like an armchair fan getting to watch this race from the most unique perspective imaginable. I had to snap back to reality as Mulsanne Corner rapidly came into view; I reminded myself I wasn't an observer, I was actually part of this race.

At the end of it all, at the end of my stint, I got out and felt like a fighter pilot coming back from the war with my plane in one piece. It was quite a journey to go through, the ultimate for me in motorsport. And suddenly I was snapped out of thinking nothing else existed beyond the car to sudden reality: a racing track with 300,000 people watching, and many more on TV. The sense of satisfaction was enormous.

As a rookie team we were seventeenth overall out of sixty and I felt exhausted but exhilarated, a long-term ambition successfully – and safely – achieved.

With the cancer diagnosis, the motorsport was put on the back burner for a while, but I still have ambitions in that part of my life. So many events appeal: I'd love to do Le Mans again one day, the twenty-four-hour races at the Nürburgring and Spa, the Bathurst 12 Hour in Australia, some rallycross, to be honest it almost doesn't matter what race it is, I'd give anything a go. I just feel so delighted to have found something else I enjoy where I can keep going fast in circles and so fortunate to get the chance to actually do it.

CHAPTER SEVEN

2024

MY visor's down, racing around Snetterton Circuit, down the Senna Straight, into Riches, then Montreal and beyond. The backdrop is a blur as I speed along. This track day is purely for fun, a rare sojourn in the middle of my chemo treatment, one of those moments where my body feels good enough to go for a drive at pace, an opportunity I seize when I can. It's the perfect distraction, so much concentration focused on keeping the car on track that for a time the cancer is not even in my thoughts. It's refreshing and so needed.

I've found these moments crucial during the last few months and planned them in as and when they feel possible. I told a small number of my cycling mates about my diagnosis, and for those who enjoy driving on track, we organised a special day in Wales in late November before the chemo began. It helped me see how essential this sort of focus was, offering an escape like no other and spending time with friends. Jamie Staff, with whom I won team sprint gold at the Beijing Olympics, flew over from San Diego, where he now lives and works. Roger Green travelled over from Portugal. Others came from closer by: Jason Queally and Rob Hayles, Mike Hunter, John Morris were all there. Justin Grace, Phil Hindes, George North, Jason Kenny too, plus Phil and James Abbott from Revolution Racecars came along with a couple of very special cars for us to enjoy.

Craig MacLean, another good mate and former teammate with whom I won my first Olympic medal all the way back in 2000, couldn't make the track day. But he had flown in a few weeks before from his home in Switzerland with his partner, Emily, as soon as he heard about the diagnosis. All round, I have been blown away by this practical and tangible display of support not just from these guys but from all my friends. Throughout the last few months, since I told each of them privately about my situation, they have all been incredible in their individual ways, remaining in constant contact, their partners also reaching out and supporting Sarra. I could not let this moment pass without acknowledging my appreciation of them. I have heard some say that a cancer diagnosis changes lots of things, including friendships. In my particular case, the depth of support, understanding and empathy they have shown to me and to Sarra has deepened them to a level I couldn't have imagined.

As I pull into the pits, I slip my phone out of my pocket and begin to scroll through it. I've had two or three missed calls from an old friend. We've not seen each other for some time bar maybe exchanging the odd message, so the calls are somewhat unexpected. Before I have a chance to call him back, Sarra calls. I answer immediately, because she is at a medical appointment herself. She insisted it was better for me to do a track day than see the inside of another hospital, potentially surrounding myself with more sick people, but I feel guilty that I'm not with her, so I make sure I answer as soon as she calls.

She sounds a little twitchy, as she explains that our friend has been calling because a journalist has been asking him whether it's true I have a 'terminal' illness. The news sends a shiver down my spine – this is the start of the moment we knew would come, but I'd been so far away from my worries that morning, I'd forgotten.

I call the friend back, and he's all in a fluster. He says, 'I've heard a rumour that you're terminally ill.' 'What do you mean?' I reply. 'Who said that?' I'd not told him the news. I feel bad this is how he's hearing about it, through whispers and rumours, as it were, rather than straight from me. He sounds panicked and a bit lost.

I knew this day would come, that somehow the news would leak out. As for where and how it's leaked, I have absolutely no idea, but I need to get on the front foot. If there's going to be an article about me, I want it to be accurate because if misinformation gets out, the damage is already done. What's the phrase, 'A lie can travel half way around the world while the truth is putting its shoes on'? For the sake of the children, I need information to at least be accurate.

So, from the Snetterton pits, I make a plan with Sarra over the phone. We make immediate arrangements to prepare a press release. Oddly, reading the first one I drafted in the earliest days of my diagnosis again, it's encouraging to think how much I've already progressed both physically and mentally since that point. The statement needs a fair bit of redrafting: the words don't reflect where I am now. I also realise I don't have to share everything. I don't need to publicly state that it's a Stage 4, incurable illness. That information can wait. As the new mantra in our household says, 'not here, not now'. That piece of news is for another day.

The revised draft is more positive, while at the same time trying to make it clear to people that this isn't something trivial. It's serious, as I'm in the midst of a course of chemo-therapy, but I want the message to be upbeat, that it is business as usual and I am still working through it. Most importantly, it states clearly that I don't want more questions around it for the sake of my family. I don't want the press – or even kind-hearted strangers – to ask what my prognosis is. I don't even want people to ask what type of cancer it is. I can only do this in little steps, and I want to take it slowly as we are all still processing it as a family and as individuals. By the time Sarra and I finish drafting the press release, I am feeling upbeat and almost liberated that I can finally relieve myself a little of this huge burden I have been carrying, and I feel ready to share it.

I have a bit of news. Last year, I was diagnosed with cancer, which came as a huge shock, having had no symptoms up to that point. I'm currently receiving treatment, including chemotherapy, which thankfully is going really well. I'd like to extend my sincere gratitude to all the medical professionals for their amazing help and care. For the sake of my young family, I had hoped to keep this information private, but regrettably our hand has been forced. Whilst I'm thankful for any support, I'd like to deal with this privately. My heart goes out to the many others who are also going through similar challenges right now. I'm optimistic, positive and surrounded by love, for which I'm truly grateful. As you might imagine, the last few months have been incredibly difficult. However, I currently feel fine – I am continuing to work, ride my bike and live my life as normal. It's an exciting year of work ahead, not least with the Paris Olympics in July. I can't wait to get stuck in, have fun and share it with you all.

My finger hovers over the button on my phone for a long time before I post it on Instagram. As with my retirement, it feels like it isn't a reality until I say it (or post it, in this case). I know things will change from the instant it becomes public knowledge. Until now, we had cocooned ourselves with no one knowing, beyond family, some friends and the medics taking care of me. I feel as ready as I will ever be, so I press send . . . and then out it goes, a silent delivery to the wider world. As soon as I do so, I am consumed once again with the grief and horror of my diagnosis. The emotions and memories of that day back in September come flooding back to me and I feel shattered by it all over again.

Once the statement goes out on Instagram, it takes off. It's a reminder of how powerful social media is. Things go absolutely crazy. I have already turned off notifications to that specific message but people reply to other social media posts of mine too, wishing me well, and my mobile phone repeatedly lights up with texts and emails from a wealth of friends and acquaintances. I feel guilty for those I hadn't told yet because they have to go through the shock of hearing it from my generic statement to the wider public. I'd like to have told everyone in my life either face to face or via a message, but that just wasn't possible because we were trying to keep things private and life was moving too fast.

This is real and everyone knows about it now is the thought that goes round and round, along with the uncertainty as to how everyone will react. What happens at school drop-off or pick-up for the kids? What about when I'm giving a talk at an event, or heading to a track day, or even just popping down the shops? Am I obliged to talk about this everywhere I go? Does this now define me? Now it's out there, what happens next? Will I be met by paparazzi trying to dig deeper and attempt to uncover more information about my cancer? I have a fear the press will want to get a picture of me to see whether

I've lost my hair and quite how badly the cancer might have ravaged me. I've readied myself for these possibilities – I've had weeks and months to prepare for this point – yet I'm shocked at just how much sharing the post unravels me. I am bereft once again, having to face the reality of the situation I'm in, with the world now knowing that I have cancer. I know, deep down, that the wider world knows nothing more than what I have said in my statement and that they probably don't give it much thought anyway, but *I* know the full truth, which is that the diagnosis is catastrophic, and now I'm reckoning with it.

Alongside these worries and questions I am trying to deal with, the reaction from friends and strangers makes me feel deeply loved and, at times, overcome with emotion. There is a vast array of messages stretching from friends going back to my school days matched with messages from countless strangers, people I've never met or heard from before, simply wanting to wish me well. It is kind, thoughtful, touching, heartwarming. When I get on the bike on Zwift at home, I receive messages from people there too, even people I'm close to, all well-meaning and so gratefully received. I want to reply to them all, but it's just too much to contend with. People are sending the most lovely messages wishing me well and about what I mean to them. It feels like I'm reading my own eulogy and I'm thinking, *things must be pretty bad for me if this is the reaction!* I keep having to remind myself that very few of them know the full story; I wonder what their reaction would be if they did.

Some friends don't get in touch at all and when in due course they do, they tell me they didn't feel they should because we asked for privacy. I want to laugh – *not privacy from our friends, you numpty!* – but I am still very touched by their thoughtfulness. The kindness of our friends – close friends, long-term friends and even new friends – is remarkable. They send messages and, receiving no reply from either Sarra or me, they send another, not to chase us up but just to say they are thinking of us. Messaging without expectation of reply is the most helpful thing: the knowledge that someone is thinking of you but not expecting you to react in return, giving us space. Grant, who was best man at our wedding, is among the many who phones and phones me; each time he leaves a message making it clear there is no pressure to answer the phone when he calls or to even reply. He explains that I'm perpetually in his thoughts and when I feel strong enough, we can finally chat.

We have friends who turn up at the door, not intending to come in or even ring the bell but simply to drop off some food or a little parcel, something like that. Other parents message Sarra and make no mention of the announcement but offer playdates for Callum and Chloe, recognising the practical things they can do to ease our days. It feels like our friends, and even friends of friends and mere acquaintances, are catching me in their safety net. I think men, in particular, aren't always great about showing their emotions and letting out how and what they feel, but this situation has led me, and many of my friends, into new territory.

Spending the track day with the cycling boys; going to see the Chemical Brothers with some really close friends; I can see how far they are prepared to travel for me and to drop everything for me. I've never been afraid to show my emotions but in these circumstances, I find myself prone to tears at any given moment. It reminds me of being a kid and having a tumble, your knees smarting but thinking you are going to be OK . . . until your mum comes over with her gentle kindness and you suddenly flip and burst into tears. These gentle, thoughtful acts make me cry.

It's an amazing thing amid the mess to feel loved, to feel lucky, to feel like me being here and staying around makes a difference to a lot of people. I realise my thinking is shifting to planning to be around as long as I can, savouring the moments as they come, not spending the time panicking that I have to fight for every one. My outlook is changing.

Within a couple of days, the initial storm of interest dissipates. It's not that people have now stopped caring, but they read the news, profess their shock, offer good wishes and then life moves on. For me, that's ideal, leaving me to get on with my life.

I feel a sense of relief that it is finally out in the open, that this secret I've tried to hide away is finally released to the wider world, that covering my face with a mask and keeping my head down as I enter the hospital is no longer essential. It feels like I've ripped off the plaster – it is done, and there is absolutely, categorically no turning back. With just the single touch of my finger, I've gone from nobody knowing I have cancer – well, very few – to what feels like the whole world suddenly being aware of it.

One of the things I learn is how much people want to talk about cancer. I felt the very same way when I was diagnosed, I wanted to shout it from the rooftops. But what is interesting is how often people want to talk about cancer to . . . well . . . people with cancer. I did it to David Smith and people soon did it to me too and I found myself listening to other people's stories about friends and relatives who had made remarkable recoveries and also those who hadn't. We're all impacted by it. We are all products of our life experiences and the stories we tell about them, so it stands to reason people want to talk about having cancer, to share their story because it helps them process it and ultimately because it might help someone. And that brings me here, sitting at a laptop typing away. I want to document and record my experience, not just to share it with others but so that when Callum and Chloe are older, I can explain to them what was happening and the choices their mum and I made at a time when they were too young to appreciate the gravity of the situation. It has not been easy to write about nor to read it back. At times I worry if I'm doing the right thing, especially for the kids when the full story comes out. Sarra and I have chosen a balanced life, not fully in the public eye, and I've deliberately chosen never to embrace the celebrity world.

But on balance, this is so much more important than just

me, Sarra or the kids. What positives can I take from this? Can I be a positive force for others? The obvious answer is in the telling of my story. I want to be able to show people that cancer doesn't have to be a death sentence, even with Stage 4, and that there's a lot of life to live. It's scary – profoundly so at points – and while that sensation has eased for me to a certain degree, it's not entirely gone away, and I don't think it ever will.

Our hearts break every day, but we are learning how to sweep up the pieces, rebuild and carry on with a smile. For people in this or similar situations, two things can be true. What I am going through – and countless others – *is* bloody scary. You can't sugarcoat that. You never think it'll happen to you and then, when it does, it's absolutely terrifying. The second thing is that life has a way of going on, and I want to stress how wonderful and precious that is. Every single day matters, and once you are beyond those first horrific few days and weeks, and have the people you need around you, you find firm ground again and can find the ability to carry on. You must.

I'm going to make the most of it and not waste the days, months or years waiting for and expecting the worst. Imagine if I live for years more and I look back and think, man, I wasted those years just worrying about dying. I can still have a fulfilling life and experience new things. There's a lot to look forward to. I believe this applies to us all, not just people with cancer. None of us really knows how much longer we have left: that is a truth whether you have cancer or not.

Right now, I am no different to anyone else. I just have more information about my future.

For most people with Stage 4 cancer, the story doesn't end on the day of the diagnosis, and I am a prime example of that. The very words 'Stage 4' are likely to conjure up a vision for many people of an emaciated, sickly patient stricken in a hospital bed in their final days. That can, at some stage, become the reality for me and many others, but right now I look fit and healthy and more importantly, coming out of the chemo, I feel that way too. When I received my diagnosis the notion that I could ever feel strong again seemed impossible.

I'm inspired by so many people. I wrote earlier about the Paralympic champion David Smith, one of the many friends who came to see me despite his own health issues. Another who continues to motivate me is the rower Pete Reed, a three-time Olympic champion, who in 2019 aged thirty-eight suffered a spinal stroke that means he now uses a wheelchair. I know he can't be upbeat all the time and there must have been many dark days – I'm sure there still are, in fact – but he is just so unbelievably and relentlessly positive. He doesn't just seize the day, he seems to wrestle the living daylights out of it. It's simply awe-inspiring. He doesn't wallow in his situation, and I won't either: I aspire to be like David and Pete.

There are parallels to my career, too. I remember Jason Queally winning that first ever British Olympic gold in any sprint event back in Sydney in 2000. It didn't matter that countless people had tried before and failed. Once I'd seen with my own eyes that it was possible it gave me belief that maybe I could do it too. He was my hero, but he was still 'just Jason', a normal guy with huge physical potential and a determination to realise it. I got to train with him every day and learn from him. Seeing him become the best in the world made me realise there was nothing impossible about this challenge, it was achievable if, like him, I was willing to work hard enough and not give up when it became difficult. All I needed was this one example to give me the belief that I might be able to do it too.

This was the mindset I was starting to apply to my cancer. Somebody has to be the statistic at the far end of the graph, the one who lives longer than predicted in the circumstances. So why not me? Like in the film *Dumb and Dumber* when Jim Carrey's character says 'so you're saying there's a chance?!', it was realising this that made me find my fight again. If I can achieve anything in writing this book, it would be to encourage everyone in this position to find their own strength. In fact, it isn't just for those facing cancer; this applies to every single one of us in our lives. Why not set a ridiculous goal in life? Why not aim for the gold medal instead of the bronze? There may not be grounds for huge optimism, having had such a brutal diagnosis at a relatively young age, but equally, perhaps it's that exact fact that will help me go on longer than these bloody statistics suggest. So I've chosen to aim for the highest target. *Somebody* has to be that person to win gold, but only if they try.

A year ago, facing what felt like an abyss, I wanted to live every second in desperation. I vowed never to lose my temper with the kids again, I was going to be the most perfect dad, husband, person I could be. Of course, I try to be all those things now, but life, dare I say it, is beginning to feel more normal. We have the ability to adapt. A few hard months on, I've achieved a better balance. I don't have to be so intense in every moment and experience. I don't have to witness every sunrise or sunset like it's my last, I don't have to suddenly learn a new language or take up the guitar. There's not that same race-like urgency. I still hug my kids until I squeeze them too tight, but it's not because I'm scared I won't get the chance again.

CHAPTER EIGHT

2013–24

'VE always been aware of the fact that when you retire from professional sport you have a limited shelf life to be in demand and in work, as your heyday slowly but surely disappears in the rearview mirror and younger, more recent stars emerge into the spotlight. Of course, there are exceptions to the rule, Sir Jackie Stewart being an obvious example, but when I hung up my wheels I definitely had the notion to make hay while the sun shone. That combined with the fact that I've never been very good at saying 'no' to things meant that post-cycling I threw myself at everything. My attitude was that previously I'd had a singular focus on one very specific thing to the exclusion of all else. Now, I wanted to sample everything else a new working life had to offer, to experience a variety of different opportunities and see what I enjoyed most. It felt like a brave new world, and I felt fortunate people wanted me involved in their various projects, so I fully embraced that.

I started my own bike brand with Evans Cycles, called 'Hoy' bikes (yeah, it took weeks to come up with the idea for that name!). I loved the entrepreneurial side that entailed.

My degree was in sports science, so I had a passion for the science behind performance and I was always curious about bikes, components and everything that made them work well, from a functionality perspective. I didn't want to simply be the face and name of something, I wanted to roll my sleeves up and get involved at all levels. So, I helped design the bikes: their geometry, their components, their style, choice of materials, weight targets, colour, whatever was needed. I tried to draw upon my experiences from riding bikes competitively since I was seven years old, and it really was a 'pinch myself' moment when I went to the factory to see the first bikes rolling off the production line, with the shiny 'HOY' logo on the down tubes. I felt real pride whenever I saw a 'Hoy' bike out in the wild, and loved to ask people on them if they were enjoying their bike and ask for their feedback. Eleven years after the launch, I still feel that now.

More recently I've been involved with some really exciting new British start-up companies. Skarper is a pedal-assist system that you can literally clip on in seconds to turn your regular bike into an ebike, and clip off again when you want to revert back. It means that you can have the best of both worlds without buying a new bike. It's been developed in conjunction with Red Bull Advanced Technologies, an offshoot of the Formula 1 team. Like most great ideas, it's incredibly simple in principle and has been designed and created by a very talented team of individuals. When the original prototype was brought to me four years ago I was blown away by the simplicity and the effectiveness of it and

I immediately wanted to get involved. I've helped to give feedback to the engineers regarding the riding experience and what the optimal setup should be, as well as spreading the word about what a brilliant idea it is.

Another great project I'm involved with is Aerosensor, a device that clips on to the front of your bike and measures your aerodynamic efficiency as you ride. It means you can do your own aero testing on the road or velodrome and find out your most efficient riding position and equipment/clothing setup. It's for any cyclists or triathletes who may not be part of a national team or professional setup and who don't have access to a wind tunnel, but who are looking to improve their aerodynamics. It basically gives you more speed for no extra effort, which has got to be the Holy Grail of cycling, and it's a way of bringing elite cycling performance to the masses. Being a part of projects like these and seeing ingenious ideas grow from concept to marketplace is hugely exciting for me, particularly when I get to play a very small role in that process and feel part of the team.

Away from the cycling world, I've written a series of books for kids. I even have my own brand of coffee with the guys from Artisan Coffee ('The Hoy' – yes, you can see a pattern emerging here) and I do public speaking, delivering keynote speeches at all sorts of events. One of the main themes in my talks is about adapting to change and the irony isn't lost on me that, with this monumental change in my life, I find myself attempting to practise what I've preached hundreds of times over the years to tens of thousands of people.

Retirement was also one of those moments where I was forced to adapt to change and I feel I've managed it pretty well; a lot of athletes really struggle mentally when transitioning into a life away from competition. I was very lucky to be incredibly well supported by the team I had built around me, to have a clear plan and new exciting and varied goals to chase. There are still things I'd love to do. I've always wanted to get involved in coaching, or mentoring in some way or another. I've been approached for a few different roles over the years but it's never quite happened as it always felt like I'd have to drop everything else to focus solely on it and give it the time and energy it would need to do well. I think it must be a hugely rewarding experience to work with young riders with great potential and most importantly a great attitude, seeing them develop and learn and watching them fulfil their promise. Maybe one day I'll end up trackside with a stopwatch in my hand, who knows?

My first experience as a full-time pundit was at the Commonwealth Games in 2014. The BBC had set up a makeshift studio on the Glasgow velodrome concourse on the outside of turn one looking down to the track. I felt like an alien being there. I got to the velodrome for the first day's action and saw all my teammates getting ready to go out on the track. I had a very sudden and very real panic of 'Where's my bike?', 'Where's my kit?' – this sense that I needed to immediately get down there and race. It felt really wrong not to be in the familiarity of the track centre with my teammates and wearing what would have been the Scotland kit for those particular Games.

So, my first thought in this new career was: 'What am I doing up here?' I spent those few days looking at the times come up on the big screen and comparing them to the ones I was doing when I last raced at London 2012. Part of my brain was working overtime wondering if I could have won this race or that. It was quite difficult to get to grips with, but I'd heard from different athletes, who'd already retired, that the first year or two could be quite trying, that different moments would catch you out and hit you when you least expected it, inevitably leaving you to question what you were doing by retiring. But I knew I had done the right thing, even if parts of my brain had yet to catch up. I was thirty-eight years old now, I'd eked out every bit of my performance, and I knew it was the right time to stop. And now that I had, there were two choices: either deliberately avoid cycling altogether, or else fully embrace this chance to keep being involved in the sport that I loved and had given so much to. I couldn't really avoid my home Games and a velodrome with my name on it, and I didn't want to. I simply had to adjust to the transition and find the fun in it.

I also needed to be grateful for the position I found myself in. Here I was not just working on TV but also acting as an ambassador for these Games, of which I was immensely proud. Each day of the championships, organisers appointed a 'Chieftain of the Village', and for one of them, I was bestowed with that honour. My job on that day was to show various dignitaries and VIPs around the athletes' village, including Princes William and Harry, and Princess Kate, and we did a little photoshoot with Usain Bolt as well.

Bolt had caused a stir at the Games when he was reported as calling the Games 'a bit shit'. Now, I wasn't there to experience that exact exchange of words, but I remember asking him, 'What do you think of the Games?', thinking he'd say, 'Great', which, to me, they were. But he really wasn't up for it the day I saw him, saying it was too cold and wet and he wanted to be in the inside and warm as soon as humanly possible. He got his wish because a couple of days later the weather changed dramatically and we all got the weather we'd wished and prayed for, glorious sunshine and with temperatures in the mid-twenties.

Glaswegians were so proud to show off their fine city, everyone seemed to be delighted to act as Games hosts and morale was so high across the venues and the entire city. It proved to be a fantastic event and an incredible follow-up to the London Games that had blown us all away two summers earlier.

The Commonwealth Games have an opening ceremony just like the Olympics, but instead of a torch to light the Olympic flame there was the Queen's Baton Relay. Her Majesty the Queen had written a message four years earlier, put it in a scroll and inserted it in the baton. It had travelled around the Commonwealth from the end of the last Games in Delhi to the start of these ones in Glasgow, finally arriving on the first night at Parkhead, where the baton would be opened for the Queen to read her message to the crowd. In a moving moment, during the final leg of the relay, the baton was passed on to me by my uncle Andy. He was into his nineties and a bit unstable on his feet, so the plan was for him to remain seated and I would bend down and take the baton from him. But Andy being Andy, never in his life wanting to be undone by any sort of adversity, stubbornly insisted on not sitting for the event. Much to the amazement of his onlooking grandchildren, he stood up, albeit a little shakily – which also took me by surprise and warranted a massive cheer from the crowd – and then gave me a big hug. It was a particularly poignant venue for him as he'd raced here at Parkhead in his younger days and was a big Celtic fan.

Once I had the baton, it was my job to hand it over to Prince Tunku Imran, the Malaysian head of the Commonwealth Games Federation. I had an earpiece from the ceremony director telling me to walk slightly faster, to jog but not too fast as things had to be just bang on schedule from a TV perspective. It was a really proud moment, standing there in my wedding kilt in a stadium rammed full of people with the eyes of the Commonwealth upon us. As I handed over the baton, I thought my job for the night was over, so I stepped back into the background with a 'phew', thinking that was me done. Then I heard a tiny ripple of laughter, and suddenly I heard in my ear a director's message saying 'Somebody help him!' I looked across to Prince Imran, who was struggling with the baton. He was unsuccessfully trying to open it in order to pass the scroll within on to the Queen, twisting the end this way and that to no avail. The laughter started to shift from a ripple to an outpouring as this guy struggled in vain on live television in front of an estimated worldwide audience of one billion people – while Her Majesty patiently watched on.

I looked around and it became abundantly clear that no one else was going to help him, so I stepped in to see if I could assist. He passed it over to me and I had no idea what the hell I was doing but realised the catch was not releasing. I gave him some advice even though I didn't have a clue what I was talking about and, despite rather than because of my advice, he managed to open it up – much to the delight of the crowd – and pass the message on to the Queen to read. At that moment, I looked across at Her Majesty and she pulled this face: it was a great image of her with a sort of mock panicky face while I returned the compliment with something similar, a really funny and obviously rather unique moment seeing the Queen enjoy the funny side of it all during what was such a formal occasion.

Then on day one of the track cycling I turned up at the velodrome in Glasgow and, despite having my name on it, I was refused entry, much to the delight of Twitter and the press at the time. Along with my BBC colleagues, I was running a bit late and the main entrance was awash with people, so getting through there would have taken too much time in the scrum of people wanting to stop to say, 'Hi', pose for selfies and sign the odd autograph. So, I tried to sneak into the competitors' entrance, get in that way, dive upstairs and be ready in time for the broadcast. The person at the door looked down at my pass, then up at me and simply said, 'You can't come in this way, you don't have the right accreditation.' My explanation that I was on air imminently didn't bear any weight. She politely and quite correctly said, 'Sorry, there's nothing I can do.'

By this point, BBC Radio 5 Live had spotted us and within a few minutes had done a news report on me being refused entry into the Sir Chris Hoy Velodrome. It was all over the media that night and sort of blew up from there. I felt sorry for the lady in question – I think people were even trying to find out who she was – but she was only doing her job. If she'd let us in that way, she could have got in trouble with her supervisors, maybe even lost her job, and there was no chance in a million years I was going to say, 'Do you know who I am? They've named this building after me' to get in. I'd rather have been late on air than cringe myself inside out saying that. Even now, the idea of it makes my toes curl. I later put a message out on social media to say it was no problem, pointing out that she was only doing her job and telling people to lay off her. I hope that defused the situation but it was one of those memorable moments that people seemed to find funny, ridiculous or a bit of both.

For what was my first big event since retirement I needed a busy Games and that's exactly what I got. There were so many cool experiences, not just the actual sport but little moments pocketed throughout the Games. I remember looking over to see Sarra hanging out with the comedian Billy Connolly and Scotland's former First Minister, Jack McConnell. Billy had long been a hero of mine and maybe of all Scottish people, he's one of the funniest people that's ever lived, and to meet him was a real thrill. I also got to catch up with Graeme Obree, the former World Champion cyclist, another big hero of mine. Rubbing shoulders with him in Glasgow was just another surreal thing to have spawned from a career of riding around quickly in circles.

As for the punditry work, it all seemed to go pretty smoothly, not because of any innate ability I possessed but because of the professionalism of the people around me. The former Olympic triple jumper Jonathan Edwards was doing the main presenter role alongside me at Glasgow 2014 and he was the consummate professional: I learned so much that week. The list of incredible people I've got to work with and still do continues to amaze me: Clare Balding, Jill Douglas, Hazel Irvine, Gabby Logan and Dan Walker to name but a few, all so impressive at their jobs they made mine easy by asking the right questions at the right time, and allowing me the chance to explain what was going on to the audience from a rider's perspective.

When it comes to the television work, I try to imagine that I'm talking to my mum and dad (although to be fair my dad does know his stuff on track cycling!) and attempting to explain to them what's going on, not being patronising with it but not getting too technical either – it's about ensuring you give the layperson an insight so they can enjoy the racing that bit more. There's often a chance to delve into the tech, science or something more specific for the hardcore fans but the information has to be delivered in such a way that the first-time viewer still knows what's going on, what a race is about, who the good riders are, what the tactics are, why the bikes look the way they do. From the very outset this was made a lot easier thanks to the people I've worked with and still do, from crew to floor managers and beyond. I simply slot in and do my bit.

There are points where you can't help but be biased, BBC employee or not. When I started in this role, I was talking about former teammates and close friends of mine and, while I could have said I wasn't cheering them on or cele-brating their successes, that would have been a lie. Of course I was! My offering on the microphone has always been about trying to give insights into the sport and the people within it, bringing the individuals to life rather than just remarking on the live action. We can go through their backstory, as well as any injuries or setbacks they've had. Katie Archibald is the perfect example in her return at the Glasgow World Championships in 2023 after the most horrific year of her life, with horrendous injuries and crashes as well as the tragic passing of her partner Rab Wardell. You need to be able to explain all that background and hopefully deliver it sensitively and correctly so people can understand the emotion of it all for someone like Katie before, during and after the event.

Just like as an athlete, the ultimate sports broadcasting experience remains the Olympics, it's the Greatest Show on Earth and always a privilege to be part of, regardless of your role. I love the adrenaline of it all, coming in, getting prepped, a cable up your back, an earpiece in and a microphone clipped onto the shirt. The countdown begins to going on air, thirty seconds, then ten, and then 'Good luck everyone, have a great show!', then 3, 2, 1 . . . LIVE, that moment where you know that you can no longer make a mistake. I always get butterflies in my stomach right before going on air and that's a remnant of my cycling career: it's the same feeling, and I welcomed it, as I saw it as getting me to the right level of alertness. I find if I'm doing a piece to camera I can often end up doing loads of takes; 'just one more' until I get it to the point that I'm happy with it. Live on air you don't have that second chance and, when it's live, you tend to make fewer mistakes and if you do, you don't dwell on it. You simply keep going.

Thankfully I've not had too many howlers live on air. I remember one time at the Rio Games I was in between chats on air and was either checking the latest Olympic results or else social media on my phone. I would occasionally cut it a bit fine, and I'd have it on the table in front of Clare Balding and me covered by papers. Suddenly, we were on air and Clare was squeezing my leg as she was starting to talk to the camera to point out that my phone was still out. I froze in that moment, took my iPhone, and slowly put it under the table like a school kid who'd just been caught out by their teacher mid-class. I was busted live on TV by everyone on Twitter. It was quite funny actually, Clare made some comment about it live on air – as ever, completely unflustered by this amateur sitting beside her – and quickly moved on from it with the most light-hearted of remarks.

I always find that the end of a major championships – be they the Worlds, the Olympics or the Commonwealth Games – is a special moment. It reminds me of being an athlete and being a part of an amazing team; I feel lucky to still be involved in this wonderful sport.

The Rio Games have to be a highlight in this second 'cycling' career of mine. Rio was my first Olympics in retirement and my first time to view it from a totally different perspective. By then, I was over that imbalanced feeling of viewing it as a rider and feeling like I still belonged on the track and could have been competitive. Come the summer of 2016, I was still keeping fit, riding my bike and working out in the gym, but comfortable in the knowledge that my competition days were long gone.

Perhaps the moment that made me realise I was fully at peace with retirement was Jason Kenny's third gold medal in Rio. He'd already won two gold medals at that Games so was on five gold medals and a silver. If he won that race, he'd have six gold medals and a silver so would match my own Team GB Olympic record. Part of me – the competitor in me – was thinking about the records and achievements: if he didn't win then I'd still be the most successful of all time out on my own. The reality was I wanted my mate and former training partner to do as well as he possibly could, immaterial of the ramifications. I was fully aware what he'd put on the line to get to this point, what his work ethic was like and how unpredictable an event the keirin final could be as he lined up for it. I was rooting for him.

He was the world's best sprinter at this point. He had destroyed everyone in the individual sprint – the quickest by a mile – but putting that all together in the lottery of the keirin was an entirely different situation. The drama had really built up before the final ride, with it starting twenty minutes later than expected due to two false starts, even causing the ten o'clock news to be delayed back at home.

In classic Jason style, he took it all in his stride and didn't let it affect him one bit. He stayed utterly cool throughout while some of his rivals looked jittery and on edge. At the restart, he got himself in the perfect position, blasted them all, cruised to the win and took the gold medal in a fashion that suggested there had never been anything to worry about. As he crossed the line, I was so, so happy for him. It was a weird moment: he'd just equalled my record to become Britain's joint most successful Olympian of all time, but I was so very proud of him and the way he delivered under pressure. His four-year build-up had been far from perfect, he'd not dominated consistently. He had managed to get himself back to top form by the 2016 World Championships in London but there were also times when he was well off the pace. He had timed his Olympic peak to absolute perfection and we were all jumping up and down in celebration.

I really do enjoy TV work and I've been lucky enough to present a number of documentaries too, as well as the live broadcasting.

Scottish World Rally Champion Colin McRae was a hero of mine and I was asked to present a programme looking back on his unforgettable career. Colin had tragically died aged just thirty-nine in a helicopter accident with his son and two family friends. It was a horrendous tragedy and the family understandably hadn't really talked to the media about it. It was five years after the accident and day one of filming took place at the family farm where Colin had lived and the McRae family still resided. I tentatively knocked on the door and we were straight into talking to the family. I was nervous: it was my first job as a presenter, and I was tasked with managing the most delicate of conversations. But they couldn't have been warmer and more open to me as I tried to be as sympathetic as possible with any questioning. It was tough, as everywhere you turned there were physical reminders of Colin, with all his cars, bikes and mementos from a remarkable life; you half expected him to drive round the corner in his Subaru and jump out to greet you. It was such an honour for me and the film crew to be invited in by Colin's wife Alison, his father Jimmy and the rest of the McRaes, to let us tell his story – as was getting to drive some of his cars. It was another one of those sparks that ignited my ongoing passion for motorsport.

Another documentary I was involved in was *How to Win Gold*, which delved into what made a very special group of

British sports stars a success. It featured Sir Andy Murray, Sir Steve Redgrave, Lennox Lewis, Graeme Obree and Rebecca Adlington, all with very differing pathways to their remarkable successes and different stories to tell. My main criterion for doing any TV is that it has to be something I'd not only enjoy making but also the sort of programme I enjoy watching – and this documentary fulfilled that, and more.

The documentary *Dream Jobs* was a passion project for me, which went out on the Discovery channel, and involved me getting to meet a variety of people with dream jobs within the world of motorsport, although clearly it was me with the 'dream job' here! For example, I got to spend time with the professional rallycross driver Ollie Bennett, and he showed me what he did. I ended up on the start line in Barcelona for the World Rallycross Championship in a 600bhp Ford Fiesta. I even picked up a single FIA championship point for coming eighteenth – technically making me a world-ranked rallycross driver! Each episode saw me meeting a professional in that specific discipline of motorsport and then experiencing driving and racing their type of car. In one episode, I got to experience being a Porsche factory driver. I competed at Silverstone in front of a 160,000-capacity crowd in the Porsche Supercup, a support race for the Formula One weekend at the British Grand Prix. Then, a couple of weeks later, I raced in a 911 GT2 RS Clubsport at arguably the greatest circuit in the world: Spa-Francorchamps.

Another episode involved getting behind the wheel of a Monster truck in Sweden at Monster Jam, an absolute behemoth of a machine, which was a unique experience. And then I went out to Poland to take part in Gymkhana Grid with the legendary American rally driver Ken Block. Essentially it was just a flimsy excuse to get into some really mind-blowing cars while talking to some of the best drivers on the planet!

A more recent venture has been my podcast with Matt Majendie, *Sporting Misadventures*. The premise is pretty simple: each week we get a comedian on to talk about his or her sporting misadventures, very irreverent and a lot of fun. Each time we're recording an episode, it's like a highlight of my week. I've always loved comedy; I often go to stand-up gigs and even count a few comedians as friends. Back in my riding career, when I went away to training camps or races and long before all the streaming services we have now, I was very particular about packing the right DVD boxsets for that trip. I always took comedy ones and I loved sharing my enjoyment of the various shows with my teammates. And I think they enjoyed it too. I remember when Phil Hindes came across from Germany as an eighteen-year-old to join our team; I made sure he did his homework and got up to speed on British humour!

I've been lucky enough to be invited on comedy panel shows and had the odd run-in with comedians. I remember in 2000, just after the Sydney Games, I went to see Jason Byrne with a few friends in Edinburgh. I was at the back buying beers when one of our group in the front row decided to start heckling. Jason asked who he was there with and he explained one of the group was an Olympic cyclist. My heart sank as I realised I was about to become the focus of a skilled stand-up comic. As I returned with the drinks and shuffled along to my seat, cursing whoever it was that chose our seats in the front row, Jason turned to me and got me up onto the stage. The next thing I knew I was on stage and removing my trousers at the request of the audience, egged on by Jason, to show the size of my thighs to prove I actually was an Olympic cyclist!

Our first guest on the podcast was David Earl, who starred in Ricky Gervais' series *Afterlife* and *Derek*, and wrote and starred in *The Cockfields* with Joe Wilkinson. He was also the writer and star of *Brian and Charles*, a very funny and truly heartwarming film – and bizarrely the reason the podcast came about. I tweeted about how much I enjoyed it at the time and Matt Majendie got in touch. I'd known Matt for many years, he was one of the sports journalists who'd covered my cycling career and whose brother Rupert was the producer of *Brian and Charles*. Matt and I got talking and, quite out of nothing really, the podcast was born.

It turns out there are many parallels to be drawn between the career of a professional sportsperson and a professional comedian: the hard graft for many years under the radar, the knockbacks, the fear of failure, the trial and error. This podcast has been a fascinating foray into the world of comedy, which I've only known as a spectator.

We've had Irish comedian David O'Doherty come on to tell us the tale of the artist Grayson Perry, another guest on the pod, who created a cycling trophy made entirely of penises when he was a budding mountain bike rider. We've had so many people have us in stitches: Jack Whitehall, Henning Wehn, Katherine Parkinson, Miles Jupp, Nish Kumar, Greg McHugh and many more, plus of course Jason Byrne reliving the story of our first meeting. But really, it's given Matt and me an excuse to shamelessly meet our comedy heroes. Long may it continue.

CHAPTER NINE

2024

THE end of chemo has long been a marker in the sand, an uncertain and potentially moveable finishing line, the end of eighteen arduous weeks that have thrown up constant challenges. And now we are getting there, I'm genuinely excited. We are on track, having had no delays, so it's the end of one chapter, and I'm feeling positive, which is a long, long way from where I started. I step out of the penultimate session knowing I've just got one more round to go and that for the first time in months, there will be cause for a celebration of sorts, even if I don't know what lies ahead of me longer term.

Chemotherapy is different for every single person who goes through it. But as I come to the end of the course, I reflect that the biggest surprise of it hasn't been the physical side effects. When you think of chemo you think of sickness, physical pain and weakness. The unexpected low blow for me has been the mental challenge. As an athlete, I always prided myself on my mental strength, and I've always been a happy guy, and an optimist like my dad. I was totally unprepared for these sudden drops in morale. There is no catalyst

I can pinpoint that triggers the sudden plummet. I had so many points where I felt physically terrible, but I could bear it; I could reframe it as the chemo working against the cancer. What I struggled with the most were the sudden sinking sensations that would hit at random, where in an instant I felt absolutely inconsolable. I couldn't identify the specific reason for this, aside from the overall horror of having cancer, meaning I couldn't plan ahead for the next one. Even when I felt like it was coming, it always knocked me for six.

The twenty-second of March 2024 heralds the end of chemo for me and a quirk of the calendar means it falls the day before my forty-eighth birthday. As I have learned, it usually takes a couple of days for the side effects of the drugs to really peak, so we hope there may be just enough time to sneak in some limited birthday celebrations before whatever's in store this time kicks off. The final treatment itself isn't so bad – nothing like round two, where I had that allergic reaction – but the odd thing is, leaving the hospital after this final round of chemo is a huge anticlimax, not the high I was anticipating for so long. While I am feeling positive, there are no celebrations as I come to leave. Despite passing it every time I've had treatment, I am not going to be ringing the bell, like in those lovely videos of people as they leave hospital having been declared cancer free.

The realisation of this drags me down unexpectedly: I know as I exit the automatic doors of the hospital that I'll be coming back here at some point. That's a daunting feeling. It could be some way off – I hope it's a long, long way off – but the reality is that neither the doctors nor I know. My cancer's still there, all the chemo can do is keep it at bay for now. The reality is that this is Stage 4, and therefore it will come back at some point. In many ways, all I can do is sit tight and wait for what's next. When that will be, I don't know. What that will be, chemo, a new drug trial, something entirely different, again, I'm in the dark. But I am here, and I know I have time: something I didn't realise at the beginning of this.

When I try to zoom out from this malaise, I realise that part of the problem is that these months of chemo have been something proactive. As hard as chemo has been, there was an element of satisfaction (and protection), knowing there was nothing the cancer could do to really hurt me while I was smashing it so hard in return. Chemo gave me a structure, a plan, a rhythm. But when they removed my cannula after the last drop of medicine had been emptied into my body, it suddenly hit me: now, the clock is ticking down until the moment it comes back.

That night before my birthday, the cumulative effects from the chemo, the drugs, the anti-inflammatories feel like they're bubbling up to reach a horrible cocktail of a peak. I feel so ill, so tired, so run-down, and I know sleep will be elusive. The sense of despondency builds as I wake up multiple times through the night. It's more miserable knowing it's my birthday in a few hours. I know I want to celebrate and appreciate it as I genuinely don't know how many birthdays I'm going to have after this one. I understand enough now to realise and accept there will be moments like this when the brutal truth hits hard again. I know this is one of those moments and I just have to hold on tight during this dip in the emotional rollercoaster.

Morning comes, and the kids are in their element, which helps rebuild that hard-won positivity. They've blown up balloons, made cards, there are 'Happy Birthday' banners hanging up in the kitchen and they are delighted to have stuck the last cherry blossom on to 'Daddy's Tree'. Sarra has even sourced heart-shaped fireworks, at the request of the kids, which they take huge delight in that evening.

I oddly share my birthday with a raft of British Olympians: my old teammate and rival Sir Jason Kenny, Sir Steve Redgrave, who held the record number of British Olympic golds before me, and Sir Mo Farah, who was part of Team GB with me in both Beijing and London. It's a freak sporting birthday shared with Sir Roger Bannister, Mike Atherton and Joe Calzaghe amongst others too. On the morning of my birthday, a package sent by Ron Chakraborty (Head of General Sport at the BBC) arrives; it's a photo of Steve and me in the track centre at London velodrome, inscribed with *'Happy birthday Chris. Great memories of 2012. Thinking of you in your latest challenge. I know you'll come through it. All the best, Steve'* . . . The picture was taken by Mat Wayne, a BBC floor manager, who was a proper legend in the BBC world. I had the great fortune to work with him in Rio and at various World Championships and major internationals over the years. He had an operation for a brain tumour some years ago but the tumour came back and, tragically, he died last summer. It's a particularly poignant and moving image for all it represents. In addition, lots of other people have sent cards, presents and messages to show they are thinking of me. It's touching, I feel loved and it's emotional. Despite it all, I can't help feeling low, try as I might.

The birthday passes, and on day five post-chemo, I feel like I'm slowly turning the corner. One thing that has helped me get through all this is the carrot that has been dangling in front of me in the distance, and now it is here at long last. Travelling abroad. I've not been allowed to travel during the treatment but they say that after this final chemo session I can.

There is still the trepidation of heading away from home, of taking a long trip, having been secluded in a cocoon of cancer treatment for the past few months. But I can't wait to sit on a plane and take off, feeling like leaving all of the clinical attention behind me. We have planned a family holiday in the sunshine and the thought of it is helping push me on. The kids are through the roof with excitement as we head towards the plane. As far as they are concerned, that is Daddy's chemo done and dusted and out the way. I choose to try to echo them, their positivity as always pulling me into the present where I need to be.

We have a flight booked to Hong Kong, for a charity dinner and Hong Kong Sevens. The dinner is to raise funds for the

My Name's Doddie Foundation, an amazing charity founded by Doddie Weir himself for which he did so much work to find effective treatments for MND. I first met Doddie, a former rugby player for Scotland and the British and Irish Lions, back in 2004 during filming for the TV show *Superstars*. We instantly became friends, in the way that *anyone* who met Doddie would. He had an infectious personality, full of humour and fun, and the fact he was almost two metres tall made him very much the centre of attention in any room. We used to catch up at rugby internationals and charity dinners over the years and I remember being so incredibly shocked when I heard of his diagnosis of motor neurone disease. He fought so bravely but ultimately lost the battle with MND towards the end of 2022. I've been a very keen supporter of his charity since its inception so it feels very important for me to be able to attend this fundraiser in Hong Kong. It's quite a poignant dinner because of what it stands for in Doddie's memory, but for me personally, there is also some uncertainty about attending an event with hundreds of other people, inevitably having to talk about my diagnosis for the first time at a public event when people are so kind as to ask after my well-being.

Inevitably, people *do* want to talk about the cancer. I'm not scared to confront it in conversation, and I try always to thank people for bringing it up, and genuinely appreciate that they are kind enough to ask how I'm getting on. People approach it in different ways. Some ask what cancer it is. Others want to know how I'm getting on and when they hear my chemo is finished, they say things like 'good, fantastic, thank God, well, good to be able to crack on and get back to normal'. That part is hard. People have been lovely, and I know it was a big shock when I announced it. It'll be an even bigger shock when the extent of it is made clear.

After Hong Kong, we head to Thailand as a family, a holiday I couldn't have imagined six months ago. I've brought my bike with me which is nothing unusual, in fact I don't think I have ever been on a holiday where I haven't taken my bike, apart from our honeymoon. This time, my bike feels more important than ever. It feels like a statement to the outside world: I am back on my bike. Having been isolated, cycling indoors – partly because of the horrible winter weather we've experienced and partly because of the chemotherapy – the prospect of that first ride outdoors feels like a release, freedom at last. I set myself the target of riding out for two hours at dawn each day, mainly to escape the incredible South Asian heat, and making it back for breakfast with the family.

As I pedal out of the resort on the first day, stray dogs suddenly appear from all sides, a cacophony of barking, an alarming array of gnashing teeth and seemingly intent on taking a chunk out of my bike or my bare leg. I grab my bike pump from underneath me and, with it outstretched in my hand, wave it around as a warning to their salivating mouths or to use for a thwack should those teeth get too close. And then, with my heart already racing from the adrenaline rush of the canine battle, I'm straight into the steep incline and my heart only pounds faster. I'm no mountain goat – track sprinters never are – and you only need to look at my body frame to see that, but I've always prided myself on making my way up any climb I've ever attempted, be it an Alpine mountain pass or a steep slippery ramp in Macclesfield forest. I can't think of a time I've ever turned back on the countless hilly rides I've undertaken.

My target is the 'Big Buddha' at the top of the hill above our resort, a beautiful white marble statue of the Buddha sitting some forty-five metres tall, surveying the island below. The landscape is stunning all the way up, once I've left the dogs behind. It's a lush green terrain, not long after the rainy season, with monkeys occasionally popping out from the trees and a chorus of birdsong overhead. It's early so there aren't many cars on the road, bar the odd tourist aiming to get up there to beat the crowds.

My first two-wheel outdoor undertaking isn't a mountain by any stretch of the imagination, only 350 metres of climbing required to get up it, but it's steep. Five minutes into the ride, my heart rate is pounding at 170 beats per minute and I'm already breathing out of my arse. Is this the cancer, the chemo, my low red blood cell count, the fact my muscles have been wasting away, or am I losing it? Probably a combination of them all, and while it still feels so good to be back outdoors on my bike, my mind is already collecting all of these negative thoughts and worries.

I keep on pedalling, head down, legs going turn after turn, *one more pedal rev and the next*, and so on, and so on:

something I've been telling myself for decades now. Halfway up the climb, there are no further gears to go to, I'm at the limit of the bike and the limit of me. It's a physical battle pedal after pedal, and a mental one. At some point it all just becomes too much and suddenly I know I can't turn the pedals over. I grind to a halt, deflated and defeated. I look up and the road continues to climb steeply ahead of me. I can't go on. I briefly catch my breath, take a sip of water, turn the bike and roll back down the hill to be greeted by the pack of hounds snapping at my heels.

I'm utterly dejected and while I try to put a brave face on it over breakfast with the family, I'm feeling really quite low. I've never given up on a climb before, and the last six months have been such a fight to find the hope and work to a place of positivity; and for all that, I can't do the thing I've done for the whole of my professional life: keep bloody going. Sarra asks over coffee, 'How was your ride?' and I say something about it being pretty hot out there, but mostly brush off the conversation. After breakfast, I sit by the pool, looking like I am relaxing as the kids splash away happily in the water but instead thinking, *what have I become?* My morale is just so low. I tell myself to park it, move on, try a different route the next day – the flattest possible, although that's not that doable here – and just grind it out. I have to get back on my bike, and I have to keep going. In hindsight, I realise that at this point I was still just shy of three weeks after completing my last round of chemo. It was a pretty big ask to make my first outdoor ride a steep one, in tropical heat. But at the time, I wanted to be free from all of the limitations that had been forced upon me for the last four and a half months.

I scroll through maps on my phone and find as flat a route as I can for the next morning's ride, with just 700 metres total of climbing, then put it aside for the rest of the day. A new dawn comes and I wheel out of the resort – again with the bike pump in my clenched fist for the dogs. While this route is still hilly at points, there's respite too, and two hours later I'm finished, happy to have ground it out and almost ticked a box in my recovery. By day three, I start to feel a little better pushing myself. By day four, a friend who lives in Phuket suggests I meet up with him and his cycling friends for a spin. Whether they are taking it steady for my benefit, I don't know, but I manage to hang on to their wheels for two hours of their longer journey time. But the Big Buddha continues to loom large over this particular pocket of Thailand, a siren call, luring me to give it one more go, if I can muster the physical and mental strength to do so.

I know I have to go back, or at least try to. I pore over the route again, buoyed by the fact that I discover on Google Maps that the point where I abandoned my ride on day one was just as the gradient was beginning to ease – albeit briefly.

I don't tell Sarra specifically what my anticipated route is, knowing this is my own internal struggle, something I just have to do. I know there's pain and suffering lying ahead of me, but I need to, *have to* go back. After the customary canine stand-off, I tell myself I need to get back to that same point as before, and then just attack it one pedal revolution at a time. But it's tough. So, so tough. Of course, though I am mentally in a better place, my physiology hasn't miraculously changed in the space of a few days and my heart rate's going through the roof. There's the briefest of respites where the incline eases off a little and I can catch half a breath. To anyone coming past, I probably look like a mad man as I try to talk myself through it: properly out loud, coaching myself with the little breath I have. I don't enjoy pain but, in a perverse way, I'm enjoying this challenge. As I grind up the hill, turning the pedals painstakingly slowly, I almost relish how truly uncomfortable I am.

This isn't like an Alpine climb, it isn't like a classic Tour de France ascent such as Mont Ventoux or Alpe d'Huez, it's barely twenty minutes from the bottom to the top, but it's one of the toughest mental challenges I've ever tackled in my entire cycling career, as ridiculous as that might sound. It takes so much concentration and self-discipline, takes just about everything out of me really, as my chimp brain keeps on desperately telling me to stop. My legs are saying I can't do it, my lungs are shouting at me to cease, my brain's flitting between assuring me I can make this and pleading with me to give up the ghost; it's all just a constant battle. And then suddenly the tarmac beneath my wheels begins to flatten out and I'm at the top, the 7am light glinting off the pristine white of the giant Buddha, already a few other tourists walking up the steps to catch the view and take photos, bemused, no doubt, by this utterly breathless, sweaty, pale-skinned Brit.

I whip out the camera almost to prove to myself for posterity's sake that I've made it, and there at the top stands the sign . . . Mount Nakkerd! It couldn't be a more apt name. I slump over the handlebars, hit by the emotion of the occasion. I may only have been an hour in the saddle, but it's the build-up to it: the five days of doubt, the previous struggles, the lack of self-belief, and finally turning the corner, getting back to myself. Of course, it doesn't take a psychologist to realise it is also the months before that: this fight for hope and how to come back to my life, the life I still have left, and see how much of it there might be.

I'm absolutely ecstatic and don't immediately get back in the saddle to head down, allowing myself time to soak up the sights and sounds and the sense of achievement. There's no crowd chanting my name, no Union Jack to lift aloft in celebration, no TV cameras watching my every move, no gold medal being placed around my neck, not even a rival to take on. Yet I have that same sense of immense pride as I did at the pinnacle of my career. I feel like I've turned a massive corner in my recovery. I'd told myself in the days before that it wasn't important if I made it to the top or not, but I realise now it was important to me – I *did* care, desperately. I recognise this as a big step forward, having been so downbeat on that first day. When I return for breakfast this time, I'm euphoric.

Cycling has always been a huge part of my life. From the kid on a BMX bike, building ramps and getting air, to mountain biking in the Pentlands in my teens, discovering Meadowbank velodrome, the realisation of all my Olympic dreams and well beyond, and then finally in retirement just for pleasure. Now it's part of my recovery, and it feels more important than ever. It's a proactive thing that I can do to help my health and that I have some control over. It's not like taking medicine where you have to passively wait for it to work; getting on the bike allows me to take the day by the scruff of the neck and push forwards. Once I'm up and out in the fresh air riding along I'm so glad I've made that choice, although I still have to grind through it at times. Arriving home, putting the bike away, coming into the kitchen to raid the fridge, pour myself a coffee, feeling almost euphoric and so glad I've been out, encouraging my body to bounce back and get fitter and stronger.

By the time we're back home from the holiday, my confidence is growing on the bike and the weather's getting that little bit better too. It means I can get out on the Cheshire lanes or even into the Peak District if I'm feeling brave, for a couple of hours usually by myself, sometimes with a mate. I'm not flying yet, but nor am I left gasping for air, and with each ride I feel like I'm digging myself further out of what the chemo put me through. I have more energy, food tastes better, my face is no longer as puffy, which was a huge side effect of the drugs. There were times when I'd look in the mirror and think, *Oh my God, I don't recognise myself.* I'm not quite back to the point where I was before all this happened, but I'm improving all the time and appreciating that feeling of being better when I know how much worse I felt before.

And as time goes on, I start to genuinely push myself. Not long after the Thailand trip, I head up to Gleneagles for a 'work' cycling weekend. It's been in the diary since last year and has been a major incentive for me to aim for, to make sure I'm fit enough to get round. It's a two-night stay at one of the best hotels in Scotland, and combined with the amazing roads, incredible food and hospitality, it's a stretch to call it 'work'.

I'm lined up to ride 215 kilometres throughout the weekend with the guests, which isn't necessarily a huge distance, but the Saturday route is likely to take around six hours. This is well out of my comfort zone in terms of time in the saddle, regardless of cancer diagnoses. It isn't a case of just riding the distance and hanging in there; as befits the ride leader, I want to be able to chat to all the guests as we roll along and make it as memorable an experience for them as I can. If my heart rate is through the roof, breathing so hard I can't speak and there's snot running down my face it's likely to be memorable for all the wrong reasons!

So I feel a bit of pressure when I arrive on the Friday, simply because I want to do a decent job, but I am not sure if I am up to it. My fears evaporate from the outset when I meet the Gleneagles team and hotel guests; there is such a friendly and relaxed atmosphere I am immediately at ease and know this is going to be a special couple of days.

That's not to say it is a walk in the park. On the Saturday

for the big ride, we are running a bit behind schedule with around 30km left to go. As part of the package the guests have massages and spa treatments booked back at Gleneagles, and it becomes apparent that we really have to press on in order to make the time slots. I ask if anyone wants a fast blast back and one guest is up for it. So we start to squeeze the pressure a bit, picking up pace, getting more crouched over the bars, pressing on with intent. Before long I am going as hard as I can at this point for a sustained effort – not a flat out sprint but the best I can manage at this stage of my recovery. Unlike the misery of suffering up the hill in Phuket, this effort is hard but fun. For the first time since this whole saga began I really enjoy myself, pushing my body, making progress on the Perthshire roads. It is so satisfying to see glimmers of hope and positivity and I feel a little bit like my old self again. When I get in for my massage I fall asleep almost immediately, Nakkerd but content.

It isn't only on the bike that I begin to feel this positivity and contentment. As the chemo effects slowly subside and I begin to see how a future might look, I find myself feeling a little more normal, a little less frantic to hug the kids constantly. Now, I feel more normal than I could ever have imagined in those first November days, and I am always grateful for it.

CHAPTER TEN

2024

CANCER is no longer the first thing I think about when I wake up in the morning, nor the thing I dream about every night. In the early days of my diagnosis, it was the sharpest of jolts at the dawning of every day, a damning verdict delivered again and again and again each time I opened my eyes. It's taken me months to be able to fully process it, and for my stress levels – which were through the roof – to begin to come down.

There was a time when I genuinely felt I would never get back to feeling normal. Now, I can be totally immersed in what I'm doing for much of my day, and crack on without dwelling on the cancer as I was before.

For that, I primarily have Sarra and the kids to thank. Any parents will know that their day revolves around their kids and is dictated by them too. Being ensconced in the family is genuinely the best part of any day, and watching the kids grow and develop as the days stack up is a privilege, though I sometimes question that outlook when Callum and Chloe excitedly bundle into our room at six o'clock in the morning! I make no pretence about being a 'morning' person – my energy levels are the absolute antithesis to theirs at that hour. Sarra's far more capable of functioning like a normal human being at that time of the day, and it usually takes a while for me to catch up.

The rhythm of our life is, I'm sure, similar to that of most other people who have children. The fast chaotic weekday mornings of getting dressed, teeth brushing and frantically packing bags and figuring out what the day has in store, be it swimming, PE, gymnastics or a trumpet lesson for Callum. Often that's the moment we realise he hasn't done his trumpet practice all week so that begins, deafeningly, at a quarter to eight, blaring away at top volume, usually with the windows wide open, and not exactly endearing us to our neighbours.

There's then often a last-minute panic to bundle the children and everything they need into the car. Sarra takes them to school – and quite abruptly, with their departure, the energy of the house evaporates, to be replaced by total peace and quiet. It's a lovely feeling initially, a moment to catch my breath before I work out what I've got on for the day while I undertake my own ritual: coffee. I love the whole routine, grinding the beans, weighing the grind, tamping, extraction, milk texturing, pouring, getting the coffee to my exact liking. You really don't want to get me talking on the subject or you'll be there for hours . . .

These mornings might be chaotic at times, but I don't want to take any of it for granted, because I still don't know what the next few years hold in terms of my health. Rather than worry about what that future holds, I focus on enjoying life as it is right now; that first sip of coffee, that silence as I miss the kids until they bundle back into the house, seven hours later.

This has been a huge and healthy shift in my mentality. Before, everything was always about tomorrow: training for tomorrow, preparing for tomorrow, working for tomorrow, both before and after the diagnosis. I still like planning ahead, looking to the future and having a purpose and a goal, but I try to immerse myself a lot more in the present moment.

Life is slower and less frenetic (the school-day mornings aside). I've needed to make that distinction with the diagnosis, the chemotherapy and other subsequent treatments. Plus, my outlook's changed. When I used to do events and days of work – delivering a keynote speech or appearing on television or having a business meeting lined up – I could find even the preparation quite stressful. Too often, I got caught up in being a perfectionist, trying to make it just so, willing it to go well and really worrying about the outcome. I still take pride in everything I do, and in the moment I give it my all, but my health situation has made me more relaxed about things I can't control. I can't entirely control this cancer, so why worry about the other stuff? One thing cancer has done for me is make me better equipped to recognise how insignificant a lot of stuff is. That early overwhelming need to do something momentous with every single remaining day, an initial side effect of the cancer diagnosis and the fact that it was Stage 4, has calmed down now. Just being present with the kids is often sufficient, and I'm able to enjoy the more mundane aspects of life and find the joy in them.

While I relish that early-morning empty-house feel, when the kids return home, the energy and noise levels of the house are restored, the way they should be. Billy Connolly's parenting tip to Sarra and me at the Commonwealth Games was 'have a noisy house', and we try to stick to that.

On the odd occasion I am home to be able to collect them from school, I do. Callum's just approaching the age where he's acting that little bit cooler, not quite as enthusiastic as he once was with his end-of-the-day greeting, a sign he's growing up so fast. I still remember as if it were yesterday when my mum would come and pick me up from school. She'd be in the car and she'd shout and wave through the open window at every boy she spotted in the distance with blond hair and the school's distinctive maroon blazer, convinced it was me. So, by the time I finally filed out of school, she'd already shouted 'Over here, Chris' at quite a few other boys. Cringe! Now I know I'm as embarrassing as my mum once was to me, or at least I hope I am. I'm glad to be: it means I'm still here to be embarrassing. That in itself is enough.

Chloe's different. She's still at that age where Daddy can do no wrong, though I'm readily aware that won't always be the case. She'll run out of the school gates and jump into my arms for a big cuddle. I'm part of a very affectionate family and I've always been one to hug my mum and dad, even as I get older. And I'm determined to hug my own children at every opportunity I can, and so far, they always hold on tight, like koalas, we always joke.

I've always been grateful to the family around me – friends too – for keeping me fairly grounded. At the peak of Olympic success, they never let me get too big for my boots, and my parents and sister Carrie have been the foundation throughout my whole career and my whole life. I've always trusted their opinions and their guidance. They've supported me through thick and thin, acting as a listening ear, keeping my feet on the ground and letting me know should I ever get out of line. We're still very close, though the relationship with my mum has changed a lot in recent years.

Whenever I go to visit her, she greets me with a smile. She doesn't know who I am now, but I'm sure there's a certain smile reserved just for me. It makes me realise there's something still there of mum, and it's such a lovely reaction to be met with. Her Alzheimer's was a really slow, gradual process. She'd worked tirelessly all her life as a nurse and had dealt with patients with dementia throughout that time, so she certainly knew the signs of the disease. She never talked about her own situation, and whether she was trying to mask it or hide it because she was too frightened of the implications, I'll never know. By the time the official diagnosis came, it was too late to do anything to deal with it or slow it; she was simply too far down the line.

It has to be one of the most cruel diseases of all. Whatever happens in life you can still lean back on your memories and experiences, which is what life is all about. My mum can't: the disease has taken that from her, from us. She might not be able to process what's going on around her, but I still can give her a hug, hold her hand, talk to her and she's still smiling. She's part of our lives still, and I am grateful for that. She's still able to feel love and joy, and for a long time she's made me realise how precious life is. With my own illness, I might not have the life I wanted right now, but her experience makes me think well beyond that and be happy for what I do have. And I'm grateful that she never had to go through the horror of finding out her son has cancer, the Alzheimer's spared her from that. She has the best life possible for her now, all thanks to my dad. He cares for her at home, almost entirely by himself 24/7, and that's given him the most important purpose in his life. He knows she would do exactly the same for him, and there was never any question in his mind about doing anything else. They moved to a more manageable flat in Edinburgh, newer, easier to maintain and all on the same level, and there he spends the whole day looking after my mum. Despite the huge challenges he faces, he's still there giving her the best care imaginable. He's the one person who knows everything about her, and because of his utter devotion to her, she is still here, with him, at home. I don't know how he does it, but he remains, to me, the finest example of a husband and father I could ever know.

My dad's the most unbelievably positive person in every situation. I sometimes think that's why they're so well suited. Throughout their life together, he's been the yang to mum's yin. His reaction to everything was always, *yep, it'll be fine*, while she was the more practical one, the realist in it all; it made them the perfect match. As a result, I never felt any real worry or stress as a kid, thanks to this wonderful couple who remain a wonderful couple to this day. It's an example of what happens when you meet the person who's just right for you.

He's had his own health battles with prostate cancer too. It came totally out of the blue, but when he rang me just before the London Olympics to tell me, he was so positive about it. He explained they'd caught it early and had some radiotherapy lined up. I remember how horrendous it was, hearing the news. I always thought of my dad as being indestructible and, sure enough, here he is, twelve years on and still going strong. Now, we compare our PSA levels (Prostate-Specific Antigen levels). Who says you can't make competition out of the strangest things?

Sarra is the centre of my life and has been from the moment I met her all those years ago. She truly is the best thing that's ever happened to me. All the wonderful experiences I've had over the last eighteen years have been as a direct result of us getting together and I'm so incredibly grateful for her every single day. Within a few minutes of chatting to her that very first evening I knew there and then that she was everything

I was looking for. I got to marry the one for me. We're so lucky to have each other and I think we make a fantastic team. We've been through a lot together and still, there's no one else I'd rather spend my time with. She is always by my side and she is my greatest supporter.

Sarra's unwavering love and support are all the more remarkable given what she, too, has faced in the last year, which in turn has had a significant impact on our lives. It started with a tingling in her face and tongue last summer, shortly before my own diagnosis. This led to a GP appointment. They weren't concerned, but, following protocol, referred Sarra for an MRI. The symptoms disappeared long before an appointment date arrived, which happened to be just seven days after my own dreaded news. So whilst in a daze of shock, she went off to the scan, saying it would be a chance for her to have a lie down for an hour, joking it was as close to a spa day as she'd get.

Afterwards, she continued to support me wholly and completely, leading me to push all thoughts of her MRI scan away, given her symptoms had long since disappeared. Then one evening in December, after the kids had gone to bed, Sarra looked serious and said she had something to tell me. I realised immediately it was something big as Sarra, always so strong in every situation, was beginning to crumble and struggling to get the words out. 'Do you remember that scan I went for?' she started through tear-filled eyes. 'Well, they think it might be multiple sclerosis.' I immediately broke down, distraught both by the news and the fact she'd received it without me there. She went on to explain they had called her and told her over a month before. It was so hard to try to compute that she had absorbed the awfulness of this diagnosis alone, without sharing it with me, in order to protect me.

I tried to let the words sink in as my mind was spinning, trying to understand what had been happening to her, all while she had been accompanying me to every one of my own hospital appointments. As with my diagnosis, she was the one to bring me back to the present, trying to reassure me, saying, 'Look at me, I'm fine right now, I'm here, I'm OK.'

MS is a neurological condition that can affect the brain and spinal cord, where the immune system attacks the protective sheath that covers nerve fibres in the body. This causes permanent damage or deterioration and often leads to permanent disability. It is incurable but treatment can make it manageable. I couldn't believe what I was hearing; Sarra, so fit and well, able and healthy was facing this absolute crisis in the midst of my own.

Christmas approached, and while we were trying to prepare for what at that point felt like it might be my last, she got a call from her consultant. She took it on speakerphone and we both listened. The latest scan had been worse and confirmed Sarra had very active and aggressive MS, and she needed treatment very quickly. I sat with tears rolling down my face as I listened to Sarra calmly telling the doctor that her husband had recently been diagnosed with Stage 4 cancer and simply saying, 'I need you to help me outrun this.' She asked some sensible, practical questions and then thanked the doctor for phoning. I couldn't quite fathom the amount of strength she showed to be able to take this news with such fortitude.

MS is not like my cancer where there's a clear-cut strategy and a tried and tested treatment plan in place. Instead, there is a multitude of treatments on a sliding scale of effectiveness and the main advice is for the patient to learn about MS and decide what is best for them. It seemed an impossibly overwhelming task for Sarra, facing so much else at that time too.

She started receiving treatment just as I was beginning to finish chemotherapy. She receives it by way of an intravenous drip, going into hospital for one day every six months to sit while the medicine is administered under the watchful eye of MS nurses. She was in hospital on the Thursday, recovered and then took me into the Christie on the Friday for my round of chemo, barely saying a word about it.

She has amazed me with all that she has faced. She has supported me and encourages me every step of the way, but rarely speaks about her own symptoms. She tries to stay focused on the here and now and controlling what she can by staying as active, healthy and strong as she can for as long as she can. She does a lot of strength and conditioning work, as she always has. My favourite thing in all this is that she has recently taken up piano lessons again, having played it throughout her life. The challenge of getting back to her old grade 8 level helps to keep her hands active and her mind healthy. Hearing her play lifts my spirits and I hope one day to buy her a baby grand piano for the front room. She says no in case her hands give up on her due to the MS, but we have to aim high. We have to have faith that the treatment is doing its job, effectively halting the MS in its tracks. There are days when Sarra's absolutely fine and you'd have no idea anything was wrong. But after a recent relapse, there are days when she struggles with pains in her arms and hands. It is hard to reconcile this is where we are together, given neither of us had symptoms a year ago.

Sarra is stoic, positive, a go-getter and ambitious. Having worked as a lawyer up until the kids were born, she had recently completed a counselling course and was going to go back to university to do a course in psychotherapy just as I was given my diagnosis. All of that has been stopped in its tracks as well as her work at Samaritans as a Deputy Director of our local branch. She has dealt with everything for the kids, their schooling, their activities, my appointments, the paperwork, the administrative side of planning our insurances, planning for the future. Her work has been completely put on the back burner. She is the epitome of selflessness, putting the kids and me before herself and always doing it through love not obligation. I'm so proud of her and the way she lives her life. She makes me laugh every single day and I make it my aim to do the same for her. We've never gone to sleep on an argument. Together we're greater than the sum of our parts.

The future is a great unknown for us both now. There are moments where everything becomes unsteady and life feels too precarious, especially if we think too much about the future and the kids. Will we be around to care for our kids, will they be OK? Sarra's treatment can only do so much and her condition is degenerative. But we find our way back from the pitfall of trying to predict the future. Sarra has found a characteristically courageous way to frame our situation, something we both come back to and feel grounded by. She reminds me, 'Aren't we lucky? Lucky to both be diagnosed with conditions they have medicines and treatments for. Aren't we lucky that science is ahead of us?' That's what we choose to focus on, rather than asking why we can't be cured.

Not every day and every moment is easy but, wow, it's so much more manageable and fun with Sarra by my side. Life is different now, but I think we've found our rhythm. This last year has taught us that life is fragile and we must treat it kindly, even if it doesn't do the same to us in return. After all, today might be the best we have! We're not burying our heads in the sand; instead, we face the worries and troubles head-on together and find ways to tackle them. That, for me, is being married. Part of a team, someone by your side, on this truly remarkable rollercoaster. And we still laugh. There is simply no one else I'd rather spend time with, whether out with the kids, on a date night for dinner, or most often in the evenings curled up next to each other on the sofa laughing at TV comedies together. If we're together, that's luck enough for me.

CHAPTER ELEVEN

2024

As I park my car outside the Lee Valley velodrome in spring 2024, there is a sense of London 2012 being only yesterday. I've lost count of the times I've returned here since that magical week, but the warmth of feeling never really dissipates. So much has changed now at the Queen Elizabeth Olympic Park: the flats where we athletes were housed in the Olympic Village are now Londoners' homes, and the whole area is still bustling with new building work twelve years on. There's an honours board around the concourse up in the stands, marking my two London 2012 golds and those of countless others.

This time I'm returning to give a talk at a conference about adapting to change and explaining how the lessons I learned in my cycling career can be applied to life beyond sport. Never has that been more pertinent for me personally. This talk doesn't relate to my own cancer story; instead it's a reflection on my career and some of the techniques I used to get through turbulent times. It's emotional being back here at a place where I once felt invincible.

The irony of the subject of my speech isn't lost on me. No

matter how well prepared we are in life, you never know what lies around the corner; change can happen at any moment. Sometimes it can happen with months or even years of notice; sometimes it comes with no warning and the goalposts move at the last second.

When I headed to Athens for the 2004 Olympics, I was competing in the 1km time trial event, known as the 'kilo', a four-lap solo time trial around the track, no heats, no qualifying, a solitary short, sharp stab at the gold. With ranking of world number one, I would be the final rider to go, having to sit and watch all my rivals post their times before I got on the track.

My morale was high and everything was going well. Just three weeks before the Games, at our final training camp, Steve Peters, then the team psychologist, asked if I had time for a quick chat. At that point, I'd really not engaged with him or utilised his expertise – if I'm honest, back then there was still a stigma to seeing a psychologist – but I thought, why not, if this could help my performance.

He sat me down and said, 'One potential scenario I want to pose to you to see how you might react is: what are you going to do if someone breaks the world record right before you go out on track?' It could be seconds before, and he asked me to ponder how I would respond. My first instinct was that I simply wouldn't think about it. But you try it. If someone tells you, 'don't think of a pink elephant', that's exactly what pops into your head. He had my attention now. 'What should I do then?' I asked in return, somewhat meekly. He told me I had to actively choose what I wanted to think about in that situation. By focusing on something constructive and positive I would effectively displace any negative or distracting thoughts. His advice was simple: whenever an unhelpful or negative or anxious thought popped into my head, I was to visualise my perfect race, in real time, from my perspective. This would help to reinforce the positive and not allow negative thoughts to take hold. I was to focus on the process of what I needed to do to produce my best performance but not dwell on the outcome, good or bad. To begin with I probably used this technique once or twice every day, but by the time I arrived in Athens and was in the velodrome on the night of my race, it was almost in a constant loop in my head, just focusing on my own race against the clock and what I could control.

With only four of the eighteen riders left to go, it seemed like Steve had a crystal ball. Up popped Shane Kelly from Australia and he smashed the world record. I remember thinking briefly, *Oh my God, I can't do that time,* but I didn't engage with the thought even when the next rider up, Stefan Nimke of Germany, went faster still. While I might have wanted to stick my fingers in my ears to block it all out, I couldn't ignore it. Then just seconds before I got on the track for my chance to become Olympic champion and realise a lifelong dream, Arnaud Tournaut, the four-time world champion Frenchman and penultimate rider, did the unthinkable and dipped inside the sixty-one-second mark for the first time in history, shattering the record again! The crowd went ballistic.

I got on the track, visor down, and focused only on what I was able to control: the next four laps. I don't remember much from the ride itself, just a wall of noise and an explosion of energy. As I crossed the line after four laps, an almighty roar went up from the whole stadium and I looked up to see my name on the scoreboard with the new record time next to it, exactly as I'd visualised – only this time, it was happening for real. I put my hand up and rode around in a daze, then I saw my family going wild, waving the banner and the flags, and it finally became real that the kid inspired to get on a BMX bike after watching *E.T.* was Olympic champion. I went wild too.

Dealing with the moving goalposts of the world record being broken immediately before my ride is a perfect example of last-second change. But we also all encounter slow change that might take months or years to fully materialise. About a year after winning that first Olympic gold, I got a phone call out of the blue that totally shifted my landscape. The kilo, 'my' event, was being dropped from the 2008 Olympic programme. I was currently training for an event that didn't exist anymore. It was an utter bombshell, and it was as if I went through the five stages of grief in a matter of minutes: depression, anger, denial, bargaining and acceptance. There was nothing initially I could do.

The choices were stark: either walk away from the sport and retire at the age of twenty-nine or find a way to adapt to the situation. It took me a good four or five weeks to come to a decision, which coincided with London winning the bid for the 2012 Olympics, and I knew right then that I wanted to be there. So, I needed a new goal and to make a plan for that, and the Beijing Olympics that would come in between. I was already doing the team sprint at Beijing, but to be part of that team I needed to be selected for an individual event too. There were two possible choices: the sprint and the keirin. Both required a level of tactical and technical skill not needed in the kilo. I decided to go for both and hedge my bets, with a view to dropping one event nearer the Games and focusing on the one I had the best chance of making the team in. I realised I couldn't keep dwelling on the past, I had to look forward. I had to find the opportunity in this new situation. I knew I had strengths from the kilo, which was effectively a long sprint, so I wanted to bring these into the new events. I never really believed at the start that I'd get to the same level of success that I'd seen in the kilo, but I was willing to go for it, throw myself at this new challenge and see what happened. I certainly never thought I was capable of winning three golds in one Games, as transpired in Beijing.

Change, while it's often scary, can be good, if you can find the opportunity within it. If I hadn't been forced into making that change of events I would never have done so out of choice. Why would I? None of us knows what lies ahead in life, but taking ownership of our situation gives us the best chance of a positive outcome. When big changes come, and they seem like the worst possible scenario, you never know, it might just be the best thing that's ever happened to you. And even if it isn't, taking ownership can help you change as much of the outcome as is within your power.

Our current situation is no different. Changes have been thrown at us, so we have to control what we can, adapt, surround ourselves with the right people and accept that we must adjust our mindset. While it seems hard to find any positives, right now I have come to realise that whilst I would never have chosen to be in this situation, I have found a whole new outlook and appreciation for life that I didn't have before. For that, I'm grateful. I've learned to adapt to the new parameters and make the absolute best of this hand I've been dealt.

Part of this adjustment includes how I deal with my prognosis – that my cancer is incurable, but manageable, to an extent. As time goes on, some of the doctors I speak to, including Steve, tell me more about the treatment I am on. It was first offered in 2011 and one in four of the men on the initial drug trial are still on it, so that's thirteen years they have survived and counting. This is my *Dumb and Dumber* moment I mentioned earlier: Jim Carrey's character asks if he has a chance with the film's romantic lead. She tells him it's 'one in a million', to which he delightedly responds: 'So you're saying there's a chance?!' This is my glimmer of hope. A quarter of those from that first trial are still here – and that's the boost I need. If they can last that long, then why not me too?

With each passing week, I progressively feel more positive. I have had some further treatment, post chemotherapy: radiotherapy on my spine which feels like light relief compared to chemotherapy. There's a little sense of satisfaction, another part of my treatment ticked off. But it doesn't feel particularly monumental, having only done one slight thing in my fight against cancer. It's like mopping one part of the kitchen floor and then remembering the rest of it is still covered in crap. But still, that particular week is done with. I now know what radiotherapy entails and what to expect if and when I'm back for more.

With the end of this treatment phase comes a notable date in the calendar during my recovery process: the Paris Olympics. Before the diagnosis, the plan was always to come and be part of the broadcasting team, and I was looking forward to it, especially after having (as we all did) to miss the trip to Tokyo due to the pandemic. My life has been so entwined with the Games, so much of it is part of my identity both as an athlete and now as a TV pundit, I knew I desperately wanted to be there. As it became more and more clear that I would be able to attend and present for the BBC, I found this news helped lift me through the radiotherapy and tiredness afterwards. As my health settled, the biggest risk in my mind was that I would come to Paris and feel very emotional, and that it would be too much to cope with. I needn't have worried. It surpassed all my expectations, helped all the more by getting to experience it with Sarra and the kids who came out with me.

The kids aren't really old enough to truly understand what an Olympics is, let alone what it means to compete in one. As a family we have never really talked much about my past life; the most they understand is from other kids at school who tell them that their mummy or daddy watched me in London. The kids don't care what I've done in the past, they just want me to be their dad, nothing more, nothing less. It's the same with a lot of athletes. I had the pleasure of interviewing Andy Murray for the BBC in Paris after his Games were over and his career at an end, and we had lunch the day after his final match. He was telling me how he'd phoned home to speak to his kids having just recovered from saving five match points in his thrilling first-round doubles match at Roland-Garros with Dan Evans. And one of his daughters asked him, 'Are you coming back home now Daddy?' And he had to say, 'No darling, we're through to the next round.' That sums up a young child's mentality. All they want is their daddy with them, be that tickling them, playing with them at home or reading them a bedtime story. The kids don't care what you're doing, they just want you to be their dad.

By bringing them out to Paris, Callum and Chloe finally got a bit of an understanding of what an Olympics is all about. They also began to put together the jigsaw pieces of me cycling in a velodrome and the Olympics. I realised before we left that we needed to do this because the other day Chloe asked me, 'Daddy, did you get your medals for driving in Formula One?' Before that she apparently told her class I got an Olympic medal for going upside down on a rollercoaster thirteen times at Alton Towers, so you can appreciate, I had a bit of work to do!

During the Games, lots of people came up to ask for pictures or else an autograph. The kids are used to this, but not to this extent, and they didn't want to share me with random strangers. They were perplexed by it and I found myself trying to explain why people might want a selfie with me. I was at a bit of a loss to be honest, but told them it was a privilege for me when people asked. Callum began to get it a little more when he got to meet gymnast Max Whitlock and it was his turn to ask for a picture with Max.

After the strangeness of Tokyo, where I was commentating from Salford in the middle of the night due to the time zone difference, Paris has been every bit the real Olympic experience and I have loved seeing and fully embracing this other side to my career. It was wonderful to be back again and enough time has passed both from the end of my career and also the cancer diagnosis for me to feel fully present.

Twelve years on from my last Games, I don't feel any desperation to be on the track, and nearly a year on from that first appointment, I have emerged from the depths of despair, and been able to reflect on the amazing global entity that is the Olympic Games and the role I've played in it. I can appreciate how lucky I have been to be part of it as an athlete and to continue to be part of it through broadcasting, telling the story of sport. The Olympic Games is said to be the greatest show on earth and I think that's true. It celebrates humanity, bringing all people together, regardless of politics and wars, and shows sport as a metaphor for life. The Games brings out all the highs, the lows, the bittersweet moments, passion and joy whether you are competing or spectating. It is a privilege to have been part of it and I am so pleased I was able to make it part of my life. I feel so lucky, too, sport has given me so much in life, that I've experienced so much from it and that I've learned so much from it.

It's perhaps when you step back from something and look on it again from a distance that you can then make sense of all the lessons you have learned – from frustration and disappointment to joy, relief and elation. In Paris, as I walked around the centre of the velodrome, I met countless friends I have made over the years, from teammates, coaches, rivals, colleagues, the barriers all came down and we were just one group of people who shared the same experiences from a different position. Riders such as François Pervis, Gregory Bauge, Theo Bos or Max Levy: they're the people that were on the track in those same moments as me, who shared that experience I had. They saw it from the opposite perspective but regardless of the outcome, we shared it together; you see there is that glint in their eye and moment of recognition that they remember. It was wonderful to be back in the track centre, where the sense of belonging and camaraderie is always so strong.

Once you're an Olympian, you're an Olympian for life and as I leave Paris, I already can't wait for the next Olympics, in Los Angeles in four years' time and beyond that. It's been a tough year but the magic of the Olympics, particularly the magic of experiencing it with the family, reminds me again that sport is not about medal counts or success or victories but about the lifelong connections with the people around you. That is the power of sport. Life is not here to be won or lost. It's here just to be lived.

Back home after an incredible experience in Paris I come home keener than ever to share my diagnosis publicly. Increasingly, I realise the message I want to share is that Stage 4 cancer doesn't necessarily mean an immediate death sentence, as I thought it did at the time of diagnosis. I am also aware that for some, a Stage 4 diagnosis doesn't give the luxury of time I have been offered. I remind myself every day just how precious the time I have is. I am determined not to waste it. I've been so inspired by the many Stage 4 cancer sufferers who are living their very best lives despite their situation. I like to think I'm already being one of those and will continue to be so.

I want to shine a light on Stage 4, hence the emergence of what I hope will be my own annual fundraising charity bike ride, the Tour de 4. I can't lay claim to the genius of the name – like all the best things, it comes from Sarra. We've been talking about it for a while, but the basic concept is a summer bike ride – hopefully from the velodrome with my name on it in Glasgow to Edinburgh – a little over forty miles to right where I was born and grew up. My dream is to get as many people as possible who have been affected by cancer, including friends and families, to participate, raising money for the cancer charity closest to their heart. In particular though, I want to shine a spotlight on what a Stage 4 cancer diagnosis can look like. I want to show that a Stage 4 diagnosis doesn't have to extinguish hope and positivity. Instead, I want to demonstrate, along with many others, that it is possible to live well and lead a happy life alongside this devastating diagnosis. It doesn't have to mean it's the end of the road, yet. I've learned of countless people are doing that every day: thriving in the face of cancer.

I hope this visual representation of the human side of cancer might give hope to others in a similar situation to help them see it's possible to adjust and find joy again.

For the Tour de 4, I hope to convince as many people as I can who are currently living with Stage 4 cancer to participate along with me, to whatever extent they can manage. I hope their friends and family will join in too, as I fully expect to get my family and all manner of friends involved – cyclists and non-cyclists. So they should be warned to expect emails, messages and texts haranguing you to be part of it! I'm excited about the potential of this event and the work we can do to help raise awareness of living with Stage 4 cancer.

There's a duality to this, though. It's not just to shine a light on Stage 4 but also to raise money. Treating cancer is so much about the finance available, and the more money there is, the more research and great work can be done, in whatever field. There are already countless scientists and researchers and even patients on trials who are already tackling this huge problematic area of cancer and I feel indebted to them all already. But as a species, we managed to tackle a global pandemic head-on – so just imagine what might be possible or just around the corner in our progress against cancer. I know there's not a cure for me, but with science moving fast I hope that we can protect our children and the next generation from what we have been through. That's the motivation for Sarra and me and hopefully others who will join us on this quest. It's something I want to give my all to.

CHAPTER TWELVE

ONWARDS

IN November 2023, I never thought I'd feel happiness again, never thought I'd find real enjoyment in anything again. How could I, having experienced such devastating news? That was it, it was over, my carefree life was at an end. This last year has been the most challenging one of my life to date. But somehow here I am, and I've learned how to live again in spite of that diagnosis.

When the brain suffers trauma, it can sustain physical scar tissue. A Stage 4 cancer diagnosis, or any cancer diagnosis, is traumatic and I find this scarring detail a really helpful fact; it allows me to focus on the time it takes for trauma to heal, and to accept how gradual this healing has been. It has taken nearly a year to reach this stage now, where I can look forward to doing everyday stuff, to laugh at comedy on the TV or to simply enjoy music. In those first few months, music was too triggering; it was either too nostalgic, reminding me of days long gone, or too mournful, morbidly forcing me into considering what playlist I would choose for my own funeral. Comedy just wasn't funny; how could anyone be laughing? I could raise a superficial laugh for the odd thing here and there but I couldn't imagine being able to lose control with a belly laugh ever again.

That's all changed now. With time, the landscape has shifted dramatically in a way I never thought possible. Slowly but surely, the carefree me has emerged again, despite having more worries now than I ever had before. Sarra says I'm whistling and humming again too, something that I hadn't even noticed had disappeared until she mentioned it. The runaway freight train has been slowed and the brakes are on. We've managed to get my health into a relatively stable condition, which certainly wasn't a given at the beginning of the diagnosis.

In general, cancer is thought of as a physical challenge and the focus tends to be on the impact it has on any sufferer's body. For me, the mental struggle has been the greatest shock. I've had to find a way to strip it down, and the best I can do is this: in one short sentence my life was turned upside down. '*It's incurable, but it's manageable.*' But in actual fact, nothing's changed. I'm still walking, talking, breathing, eating and sleeping. I just happen to know more information about my future than most people might do about theirs. Admittedly, it is pretty devastating information, but I have found a way to use it to my advantage. I try not to think about what it might take from me, but instead, what can I take from it? With that, changing the power of those words, my outlook on everything has changed.

We all have a finite time on the planet and my prognosis is two to four years, so I have a rough timeline to work with.

But I hope to stay around a lot, lot longer than that. My future is at once knowable and unknowable, and I naturally think a lot about it, picturing how things will look for me and my family, with and without me in it, but also working out how to prolong my time with them.

What is helpful to remember is that the future doesn't exist, it's merely a concept in our minds which we may or may not have control over. Worrying about what might happen, trying to predict the future, is wasting your energy on something that doesn't exist. I may spend the next ten years worrying about how the cancer will see me off, but in fact my final date with destiny might be something else entirely. The reality of your life is always now. The past is a memory and the future is simply a thought. We can keep ourselves so busy looking ahead to a future which will never arrive. All we have is now. I'm becoming better at slowing things right down and not worrying about stuff that hasn't happened yet.

I'm still the same person, but my perception of and approach to life have changed. You can't go through something like this without being altered in a major way. I certainly view the world differently now. A diagnosis like this reminds you of the precariousness of life. It makes you understand what's at stake; you become better at recognising and appreciating the little things. It stops you taking things for granted and makes you understand more about love because suddenly you know what it costs.

It has enriched me. I love like I've never loved before. It

has given me the courage to express my feelings, stay in touch with friends, allow happiness to be, learn to be still. The life I have left now is a gift. I shall cherish it and live it to its fullest.

Despite everything that's happened this year, I genuinely don't feel unlucky with my lot. Instead, I try to look at the bigger picture and realise how incredibly lucky I've been in my life so far in so many different ways. When things feel a bit unfair, I remind myself not to think 'why me?' but instead 'why not me?'. This is just life, it happens to countless other people around the world, so why wouldn't it be the same for me and my family? As Sarra reminds me, we each have a treatment plan, and they're working. What more can we expect? It's made me appreciate so much more in life. Sure, I wouldn't choose for this to happen to me and if I could change it I would, but I do feel a better person for everything that's happened these past months.

Don't get me wrong, not everything is perfect, I've not suddenly achieved some sort of Buddhist-like Zen master status. There are still dark moments when the emotions flood in and everything becomes too much. Almost always, that overwhelming sense of emotion involves either thoughts of or talking about Sarra and the kids. In the early days, it was almost like a drowning sensation it was so much to bear; now when it hits me I am able to bounce back quickly. Time can seem so terrifyingly fast. Already a year has gone by since the diagnosis and that's a large proportion of my initial prognosis. I can't help myself from wondering how many more I have. That's only human nature. It is dangerously easy to get carried away in your thoughts and think that moment's going to be here before I know it. But I also have the power to slow things down, to view things differently and to enjoy the right now, and that is my choice, every time: 'not now'.

The here and now I have to see as a privilege because I have a chance – and I don't know how long I'll have this chance for – to appreciate everything. I understand full well that a lot of people don't get that opportunity. So now, I snap out of those lows quickly, always with the 'not now' message in my head from Sarra. And she's right. None of us can outrun death and time, try as we might. I'd rather live a life full of the things I hold dear, albeit a little shorter than I hoped. I genuinely believe I have had the opportunity to truly live the best life for me. I am acutely aware that not everyone gets that, and I see it as a gift. I really don't want anyone's pity or for people to look at me or think of me any differently. I want people to see where I am in it instead: in a good place. And the road ahead is filled with action, not just blind hope. I am so fortunate to feel like I've lived ten lifetimes already but I also feel like there's more to live and to look forward to.

None of us knows how long we're going to be around for, me included, but we can all alter our outlook for the better. It isn't necessarily about positive thinking either. You don't have to bounce out of bed each and every morning with a 'this is amazing' attitude. Every day doesn't have to consist of thinking everything is brilliant. Instead, simply taking an approach of not being negative and trying to avoid thinking 'poor me' is enough. There's a middle road, and I've become good at willing myself there, of not dwelling on and wallowing in a particular situation, but not forcing myself to pretend nothing has happened either. Cancer was an uninvited guest and now it stays with us. I choose to face it, acknowledge and recognise it. I can't chase it away but I can choose how I approach each day. It's a commitment, something I consciously practise. I choose to influence my life and allow my attention to focus on the good, and the present. And now, it not longer controls my every thought.

I'm just out here trying not to be negative, simple as that. And for now, it's working. The happy ending to this story is that I continue to be the person I always was despite these drastic changes taking place. I'm not naïve or stupid. I know what the diagnosis means but, at the same time, I feel there are glimmers of hope and that's all I need really, something or someone to tell me that this is possible. I'm focusing on doing everything I can to look after myself and put my faith in medical science. There are amazing people all over the world researching and coming up with ways to tackle cancer, MS, all sorts of diseases we currently think of as incurable. This isn't just for me but for people well beyond in the future and it's a glimmer of hope I like to hold fast to.

I also want people reading this who have just had their own damning diagnosis – be that cancer, another illness or something else altogether – and their friends and families – to know that you can find a way through. Getting through that initial phase will be painful and that pain, that horrific first moment, will never go away, but you'll get to a point where you come out the other side and you can push on, however that may look to you. Hold onto any part of your story that reminds you how lucky you are, accept what you can't change and live in the moment.

I am determined to change perceptions about Stage 4 cancer in particular. At the Tour de 4, I'll be there with other people in the same boat as me for as long as I can. And I hope if someone's reading this or watching the Tour de 4 in the future they'll think, 'Oh, Chris Hoy's still there, riding a bike! I hope to change the understanding of cancer and remind people of what they can still do. I hope people take comfort from that.

And now, a word for Sarra, Callum and Chloe.

I never would have achieved anything without Sarra. I am nothing without her. All the best parts of my life came about because I met her. I never feel that what I say or what I write about her is enough, it always seems insufficient when I read or hear it back, but I want to try.

She's been everything to me, and continues to be everything to me, and I can't believe how lucky I am that we stumbled into each other's lives. She knows every part of me; the sad me, the heartbroken me, the happy me, the determined me, and she's been by my side throughout it all, my one constant.

Our love is unconditional. She's the most remarkable person I could ever have hoped to meet: selfless, loving, caring, hilarious, intelligent, beautiful, so bright and capable at everything. With her by my side, however bad things might get, anything seems possible. When you tell her something you always feel seen and heard. She actually listens. She stands out from all the rest. Hearing her let out a genuine raucous laugh puts me in a good mood on the spot. All my happiest memories are with her and I know we have many more to make together.

I love you with all my heart, Sarra.

One day Callum and Chloe will read this book and while I'm sure it will be painful for them, my hope is that they don't dwell on the sadness but instead focus on the love surrounding them.

Their existence has extended my spectrum of emotions and amplified them to a degree I never knew possible. My mum used to say to me when I was a kid that you only understand the love of a parent when you become one, and I now know how right she was. The worry and fear I felt when they were unwell as babies, the pride in watching them develop, learn and grow, the reflected joy I feel when they experience happiness are on a level beyond anything I could have imagined prior to them coming into our lives.

I hope to be around for many more years to come to continue witnessing these moments and so much more. I can't promise to be around for all of their lives, but I can promise to love them for the rest of mine.

My advice to them both is to live life with a smile on your face. Try to find the fun and joy in any situation, and to follow your passions. The world is a big place, go out there, find out what you enjoy and give it everything!

Aim high – have ridiculous goals – but don't let those ambitions weigh you down. Use them to inspire you to make the most of every day, but don't be too hard on yourself – failure is where the important lessons are.

Don't compare yourself to others – the only person you should measure against is yourself, yesterday.

Look after your mum. She's the best person I've ever met on this planet. We are all so lucky to have her in our lives and she will give you hugs from me.

I hope that you will always feel the unconditional love and pride I have for you and know that you brought sunshine into my world, simply by being yourselves.

Without realising it, you've both given me so much strength during these most difficult times and even in the darkest moments you've made me laugh and given me hope.

I'm so lucky to be your dad, I couldn't have wished for a better son and daughter. You made me a better person and brought so much joy into my life. It's impossible to express exactly how I feel about you both, but just know that you make me grateful for every second I have with you.

When you feel sad or lonely, know that wherever you are or whatever is happening in your life at that moment, I'm there and I'm surrounding you with love.

I read this poem out at Callum's Blessing when he was still a baby. I think it's lovely and I hope both Callum and Chloe continue to enjoy it too:

Follow Your Dreams
by Jim Boswell

When others say, 'It's hopeless and it really can't be done.'
When they tell you, 'It's all over. It's a race that can't
    be won.'
And they promise, 'You could spend your life just
    lying in the sun.'
Follow your dreams, boy. Follow your dreams!

When the people you admire, but who wouldn't
    understand,
Tell you, 'Other roads are safer. Your dreams are much
    too grand.'
Or the doubters and the tempters try to take you by
    the hand.
Follow your dreams, boy. Follow your dreams!

You should listen to the counsel of the people that
    you trust.
But don't be turned aside just because they might
    get fussed.
You live the life that in your heart you know you really
    must.

Follow your dreams, boy. Follow your dreams!

There is nothing you can't conquer if you believe you
can.
No mountains you can't straddle, no oceans you can't
span.
Just conjure up a vision and set yourself a plan.
Follow your dreams, boy. Follow your dreams!

ACKNOWLEDGEMENTS

IT'S hard to know where to start when writing the acknowledgements for any book but it's particularly difficult for a book like this, which has documented such a testing time in my life.

It's often in tough times that people are given an opportunity to demonstrate how amazing they are. There are so many who have gone above and beyond in supporting me, Sarra and the kids. Doubtless a list will never be comprehensive and I know the moment I send it to the publishers, it'll dawn on me that I will have forgotten someone deeply important, simply a reflection of how much is going on in my head right now.

Top of the list are my family, my Mum and Dad, my sister Carrie and her family, together with my extended family including my aunties, uncles and cousins. My mother- and father-in-law Rosie and Bob who along with my sister-in-law Rachel have been a huge practical and emotional help to us on top of everything else.

In addition, huge thanks to my family and close friends who have carried the heavy burden of knowing the full extent of my illness. They have supported me while dealing with their own worries too. Thank you.

To all of my friends who have helped guide me through this, none of whom I could be without – thank you to each and every one of you.

I want to name a few people in particular who have helped me more than they might realise and who might be unaware of how big an impact their gestures or actions have had: Phil Abbot, Becky Adlington, Mohsin Altajir, Amin Aminian, Marco Attard, Ean Brown and the guys at Skarper, Martin Brundle, Phil Burt, Ron Chakraborty, Laura Cibulskaite, Humphrey and Nicola Cobbold, Helen Dapre, Jill Douglas, Louise Duffy, Callum Duncan, Sophie Fairbanks, Sean Fitzpatrick, Grant Florence, Sarah and Chris Ford, Fiona Foster, James and Debs Gammell, Susannah Gammell, Graham Glen, Justin Grace, Keren Grant, Melanie Greaves, Roger Green and Janet Mills, Rob and Vicky Hayles, Phil Hindes, Mike Hunter, Peter Jacques, Gethin Jones, Jason Kenny, Tom Kitchin, Kelly McAulay and Matt Deakin, Jo and Rich McCabe, Craig Maclean and Emily Smith, Sara McMahon, Dickie Meaden, Stephen Moon, John and Sam Morris, Martin Murray, Jon and Carli Norfolk, George and Becky North, Lucy Oldham, Jonathan Palmer, Ashley Palmer Watts, Victoria Pendleton, Lee Penson, Mark and Clare Plunkett, Nina Ponsford, Jason Queally, Kirsty and Gillan Rankin, Steve Redgrave, Pete Reed, Charlie Reid, Caroline Robb, Rhona Robinson, Tom Rowlands, Ross Simpson, David Smith, Jamie Staff, Nicola and Rich Stones, Andrew Thomas,

Kerry Trewern, Mark and Claire Urquhart, Becky Williams, and Rob Woodhouse.

Thanks to all of the staff at the Christie for their ongoing support and help. Thanks also to James Wylie, Emma Overend, Ged McDermott, Nick James, Chris Evans, Pete Speake, Ros Eeles, Andy Taylor and Steve Peters.

To Matt Majendie, for all his hard work in helping me write this book, and to the *Sporting MisAdventures* weekly distraction for the fun we have and hopefully much more to come.

Thanks to all at The Blair Partnership, especially Neil Blair, Rory Scarfe and Emily Barrett. Huge thanks also to Susannah Otter, Becca Mundy, Lucy Buxton and Vicky Palmer at Hodder & Stoughton.

Finally, thank you to those of you who have supported me from afar, cheered me on over the years and who continue to support me. Thanks to those of you who got in contact with me to wish me well. I read every message and took great comfort from them, and I look forward to meeting you at one of the Tour de 4 charity cycle rides!

PICTURE ACKNOWLEDGEMENTS

Family collection: 4, 6 above, 7, 8 above. Associated Press/ Alamy Stock Photo: 1 above, 2 centre right. Avpics/Alamy Stock Photo: 5 above left. Getty Images: 3 above right/Ian MacNicol, 3 centre left/Richard Heathcote, 5 centre right/ Ker Robertson, 5 below/Tom Jenkins. Kelly McAulay: 6 below. Phil O'Connor: 1 below. PA Images/Alamy Stock Photo: 2 above. SWpix.com: 3 below/Alex Broadway/Shutterstock, 8 below/Alex Whitehead/Shutterstock. Wenn Rights Ltd/Alamy Stock Photo: 2 below left.

RESOURCES

Prostate Cancer UK
www.prostatecanceruk.org

In addition to information and advice, Prostate Cancer UK offers an online community and support group where you can talk to others with prostate cancer.

They also have a helpline run by specialist nurses you can call on: 0800 074 8383 and there is an online risk checker where you can check your risk in just 30 seconds and seek advice.

MS Society
www.mssociety.org.uk

MS Society offers a mix of paid staff and volunteers, MS nurses and other experts.

Helpline: 0808 800 8000 (Monday to Friday, 9am to 7pm)

Bliss
www.bliss.org.uk

Bliss offers support to parents and families of premature or sick babies, through a wide range of free services including a video call support service.

Alzheimer's Society
www.alzheimers.org.uk

If you are affected by dementia, worried about a diagnosis or if you are a carer, trained staff are ready to give you the support you need.

Helpline: 0330 333 0804 (Monday to Wednesday, 9am to 8pm, Thursday and Friday, 9am to 5pm, Saturday and Sunday, 10am to 4pm)

Uncle Andy's book

Tomorrow You Die: The Astonishing Survival Story of a Second World War Prisoner of the Japanese by Andy Coogan